Kindergarten Teacher's
Activities Desk Book

Kindergarten Teacher's Activities Desk Book

MABEL EVELYN MILLER

PARKER PUBLISHING COMPANY, INC.
WEST NYACK, NEW YORK

Library of Congress Cataloging in Publication Data

Miller, Mabel Evelyn.
   Kindergarden teacher's activities desk book.

   1. Kindergarten—Methods and manuals.
2. Creative activities and seat work. I. Title.
LB1169.M56   372.1'3   74-9731
ISBN 0-13-515254-2

Printed in the United States of America

I dedicate this book to my sister, Leta Whitacre, who has just retired after fifty years of teaching.

The Many Ways This Book Will Help
the Kindergarten Teacher

This *Kindergarten Teacher's Activities Desk Book* is full of projects, activities, games-that-teach, classroom ideas and materials that have been thoroughly researched and tested by the author. The materials will supplement any teaching program in the kindergarten, and are detailed, explicit, and easy-to-follow, with clearly defined teaching goals. These materials cover a wide range of subject matters of vital interest to children, and will answer many of their questions about the world around them.

You can never offer young children too many learning opportunities! The more a child is exposed to interesting materials of all kinds, properly presented, of course, the more he learns, and the greater is his motivation for learning. Young children like to be kept "on tiptoe," eagerly reaching for new, unheard-of areas of interest to investigate and explore. Each day a young child should arrive in the kindergarten room with the spoken, or unspoken, question, "What are we going to do today?"

The author has found that children genuinely enjoy learning about new, unfamiliar things, and we need to develop more of the interests of our own pupils. When a child brings to school some fascinating object, and remarks, "Look what *I've* got!" the aroused interest of his classmates can be developed into an enthralling study of the object itself and related subjects, which involve every kindergartner in the classroom.

All activities, projects, games-that-teach, and ideas for developing children's interests in every area of learning have been carefully selected to make them interesting and challenging. Most of the teaching materials can be taught exactly as they are presented here.

Some materials, as in chapter 7, 11 Exciting Nature Projects That Teach Kindergartners How to Discover and Enjoy the World Around Them, may also be adapted to the learning needs

5

and interests of a particular kindergarten group. *All* materials have been teacher-tested for use in every phase of the kindergarten program. Experienced teachers recognize the value of effective, easy-to-follow methods because children enjoy such activities while acquiring new knowledge, basic skills and, often, a whole new awareness of their world.

The projects and activities cover a wide range of interests. They will involve the kindergartner with all his senses and challenge his need to participate personally in school activities. They are planned to build a young child's self-confidence and self-esteem; to help him become a better citizen and student as he realizes his own learning potentials; to increase his vocabulary, his attention span, and his ability to listen with understanding. The dramatizations, art projects, and rhythms will teach the kindergartner to creatively express his ideas and feelings.

Detailed instructions are included for making inexpensive aids and equipment for the classroom. Many materials have been included that can be effectively used for slow learners.

Use this book many times a day as a practical, always-ready helper that can make *your* classroom more interesting, more productive of real learning ... and more fun.

Mabel Evelyn Miller

Acknowledgments

I deeply appreciate the help and encouragement of many teachers who have used and approved much of the material in this book.

Contents

chapter one

31 Ideas for Making Effective Teaching Aids and Classroom Display Areas

Teaching Aids to Make Before School Starts

1. Make a Permanent Calendar

Use a metal, asbestos-backed stovetop cover. Choose a white or light yellow one, about 17" x 19" in size. This can be purchased at hardware or department stores.

Use a permanent waterproof, smear-proof black marking pen for marking lines on the calendar. Leave a 4- or 5-inch space across the top, then mark the calendar spaces.

Attach fasteners to the back of the calendar so it can hang on the wall, be used on an easel, or stand upright when leaned against a large object.

Calendar cards. Make 3" x 8" cards from cardboard or oaktag. On these cards print the names of school-year months. Decorate each card with seasonal decorations, or attach decorations on either side of the month name. Make number cards 1-31, the same size as the calendar spaces.

Buy a flexible magnetic strip at any variety store or hobby shop. This is not expensive. Cut small pieces of magnet from the strip as needed and attach them to the four corners of the month-name cards. Two small magnet pieces will be sufficient to hold the letter cards to the metal surface of the permanent calendar. Use these magnet pieces on the backs of any felt objects to be used on the calendar.

Make other objects to be used for special events or holidays such as: several pink birthday cakes with six candles on them; pumpkins, witches, or black cats; turkey; Santa, gift package, or fir tree; six-pointed snowflakes or snowmen; flags and valentines; shamrocks or kites; rabbits, or Easter lilies; birds, young animals, and spring flowers.

These decorations can be cut from felt, gift wrapping paper, or magazines. They can be made from stickers, which come in packages, and they can be drawn by the teacher. If paper is used, paste it on cardboard before attaching a small piece of the flexible magnet.

2. Make Many Cards of Various Sizes

Use heavy cardboard or oaktag; 3" x 4" cards are an excellent size for alphabet letters and numbers. Make several cards for each letter and number from 1-10 with a black felt-tipped pen.

Make 3" x 7" cards for the children's names. These can be printed when they are enrolled.

Make 3" x 7" cards for each color name: blue, black, brown, orange, yellow, red, green, and purple. Print each color name with a felt-tipped pen of its own color.

Make enough 9" x 12" cards for the entire kindergarten enrollment, so each child may have one to use when learning colors. On these large cards print the names of the above-mentioned eight colors found in the kindergartner's crayon box. Print each color name on the card with a felt-tipped pen of its own color.

Suggestion: If there is a paper salesman in the area, contact him about surplus paper. He often has stacks of cardboard samples, which he will probably give to teachers. These samples make excellent cards to be used in many teaching aids.

3. Make a Flannel Board

Use one side of a large corrugated paper box. Cover it with felt. Heavy outing flannel can also be used. If a frame is desired, edge the flannel board with braid from the sewing counter of any notion store.

Cut out all kinds of small shapes from assorted felt pieces, to be used in number games. Figures can also be cut from construction paper, but must have a piece of felt glued to the back so they will adhere to the felt board.

Suggested shapes are rabbits, squirrels, puppies, cats, teddy bears, dogs, clowns, snowmen, birds, stars, pine trees, boy and girl figures, Indians, seals, Eskimos, fish, boots, shoes, hats, mittens, hearts, apples, pears, bananas, carrots, pumpkins, and so on.

If a teacher has no special drawing skill, she can get ideas for these figures from children's books found on shelves of variety, department and some grocery stores. Pictures cut from old workbooks and storybooks can also be used.

4. Make Fruit from Styrofoam Shapes
Make Fruit from Homemade Play Dough

This fruit can be used by the teacher when teaching ways in which whole objects can be divided into halves, fourths, and thirds.

Divide Styrofoam fruit, using a very sharp knife or an electric slicing knife. Color the fruit shapes with powdered tempera paint or colored chalk. Spray a fixative on them, if desired.

Recipe for Homemade Play Dough

1 part salt.

4 parts flour.

Enough water to moisten into dough. (If desired, use cake coloring to tint dough).

Knead the mixture with floured hands on a board covered with waxed paper. Shape into fruit. Allow to dry. Paint with poster paint, acrylic paint, or enamel.

5. Make Geometric Shapes from Bread Dough

Use the above recipe for homemade dough or the following dough recipe:

3 slices *white* bread. (Remove crusts and break bread into small pieces.)

3 tsps. Elmer's Glue-All. (Use more if needed.)

½ tsp. glycerine

3 drops lemon juice (optional).

Mix these ingredients together to form a smooth dough. When making many objects, double or triple this recipe, or the flour and water one above.

Divide the dough and color with food coloring.

Roll dough between sheets of waxed paper to desired thickness.

Cut into shapes with cookie cutters, a razor blade or a sharp knife. Smooth edges with fingers moistened with water.

Let dry for at least twenty-four hours. Spray with clear lacquer.

Other uses for bread dough or play dough: Make toy shapes, put a hole in each and use them for a hanging mobile. They can be decorated with tape, braid, buttons, sequins, beads, and feathers.

Make Christmas tree ornaments from dough. Have the children decorate them.

6. Make Geometric Shapes from Corrugated Paper

Use the sides from corrugated boxes. Cut circles, squares, triangles, and rectangles from the paper. Tape the edges with masking tape. Paint the shapes with tempera paint or enamel.

7. Make a Permanent Weather Chart

A metal stovetop cover can be used, or a felt-covered piece of corrugated paper as in sections 1 and 3 above. Attach symbols depicting various kinds of weather. These symbols can be made on circles of paper with a piece of felt glued to the back, or with flexible pieces of magnet attached to the back. They should indicate days that are sunny, snowy, windy, cloudy, cold, hot, stormy, and rainy. Attach two movable hands to the center of the weather chart. These can be moved by the children to indicate the weather for the day.

8. Folders or Large Envelopes Can Be Made Ahead of Time

These can be used by the teacher in many ways. The names of the children can be printed on later, and the children can

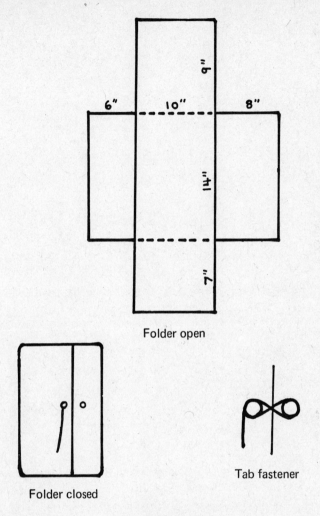

Folder open

Folder closed

Tab fastener

FIGURE 1-1

draw their own pictures on the front of the folders or envelopes beneath the printed names.

Fold 12" x 18" construction paper for both types of folders. Leave the folder open, but staple the envelope on both sides.

9. Make Permanent Folders for Filing and Storing Teaching Materials

These folders should be made from oaktag, in any size the

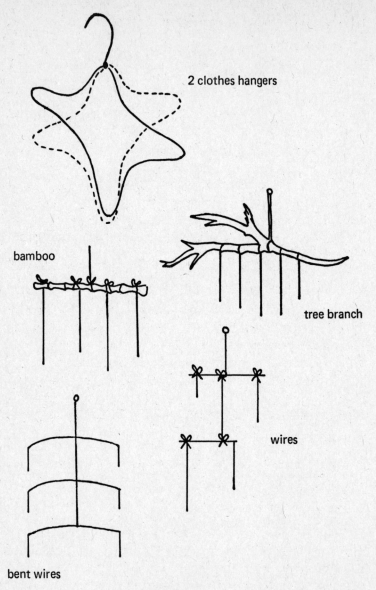

2 clothes hangers

bamboo

tree branch

wires

bent wires

FIGURE 1-2

teacher needs. The one in Figure 1-1 was made to fit 9" x 12" sheets of paper.

10. Make a Fish Mobile for the Room

Cut two fish shapes from felt, complete with fins and tails. Put these together with a bit of cotton in between to give fullness to the body. Glue the edges together. Slash the felt with scissors for fins and tails. Make eyes from masking tape and a felt-tipped pen, or glue on rolling eyes. These can be bought in any hobby shop.

Make fish from bright pieces of leather, plastic, or plastic-coated cloth, always stuffing the body with cotton.

Make fish from small round aluminum tins, which can be bought in packages. Make fins and tail from heavy aluminum foil. Insert these between the tins and glue.

Suspend the fish from a bent clothes hanger, or from bent wires. (See Figure 1-2.)

11. Make Felt Figures to Illustrate Stories

Select several short stories for children and make felt figures, or felt-backed paper figures, to illustrate the stories. These are especially effective to use at the beginning of school, when a kindergartner's attention span is very short.

Later in the year the children can use these figures to tell stories to the class. They may want to draw and cut out figures to use for telling or dramatizing a story of their own choice.

12. Gather Together a Few Old Hats!

Young children love to wear dress-up clothes. Fancy hats are great favorites. Use these hats for costumes, or to highlight a story.

An excellent use for old or fancy hats is to lend interest to the sometimes-disliked rest period in kindergarten. Allow a different child each day to wake up the rest of the children. Let the girl or boy choose a hat to wear. The type of hat can change with the month. It can represent an activity or project of current interest in the classroom. A clown hat or a bareback rider's hat, which is a bright wisp of net with a feathery plume attached, can be used for a circus theme. Boys and girls alike love to wear feathered Indian hats.

A chef's hat, a railroad engineer's cap, a black derby, a cowboy hat, and a real Mexican sombrero can be worn by either boys or girls. Officers' hats are a great favorite with children. An old-fashioned sunbonnet, or a straw hat is fun to wear. Provide a flowery hat with ribbons to tie under a small, round chin.

Whatever their choice of hats to wear while waking up their classmates, children feel very important when wearing fancy hats. Their classmates love being awakened by a child in a costume! Wearing fancy hats is a gay practice and does wonders for rest-time wigglers!

13. Make Many Five-inch Circles from Bright Construction Paper

If kindergartners have been registered before the beginning of school, print their names on the circles. Make extras for late arrivals.

Attach lengths of string to the name-circles and display them as clusters of balloons. On the first day of school, each child is shown his *own* name, on his own *balloon.* It gives the new kindergartner a feeling of belonging, because his teacher already knows him! She knew he was coming to school!

A circus activity can develop around this balloon theme. Read circus or zoo stories to the children, and have books of circus, zoo, and wild animals around for them to look at. A menagerie can be made using paper boxes with bars across the front to resemble cages, filled with small stuffed animals brought from home.

14. Make Name and Address Tags

These paper tags can be made in a variety of shapes—circles, squares, toy shapes, and so on. On them print MY NAME IS and MY ADDRESS IS. Fill in the child's name on the first day of school. Hang these tags on loops of string around the children's necks. Record the child's address on the tag and let him wear it as he goes to and from school. Each day discuss his address with him. Soon he will remember his address and the tags can be discarded.

15. Make Display Cards for the Names of Room Equipment

On each card marked "scissors," "paste," "crayons," and so on, paste a picture of the article. Cards for large pieces, such as "door," "window," "piano," "desk," and "cupboard" can be attached to the article with tape.

16. Draw, or Cut from a Magazine, the Picture of a Girl's Face and a Boy's Face

Print GIRLS and BOYS on 3" x 7" cards. Attach these pictures and cards to the doors of the girls' and boys' toilets. (This assumes, of course, that there are private toilets for kindergartners.)

17. Wind Old Yarn and String into Balls

Use these for some types of games to be played in the classroom.

18. Make Some Attractive Beanbags to be Used for Games

These can be made from bright felt, plastic-coated cloth, or regular cloth. Make them in the shapes of fish, hens, round smiling faces, rectangles, squares, and clown faces.

19. Make Minature Felt Boards

Children can use these at tables during play time.

Cut 12" x 15" pieces of corrugated paper from boxes. Cover these pieces with felt or outing flannel. Finish their edges with bias cloth tape, which can be pasted on. Masking tape can also be used for the edges.

To accompany these felt boards, supply the children with paper figures, backed with a square of felt. These figures can be cut from old books, workbooks, magazines, and toy catalogs.

Remove the top and cut one long side from shoe boxes or other boxes of a similar size. Line these boxes with felt. These can be used as rooms, a yard, a field, an airfield, a garage, and so on. Kindergartners may think of other uses for them.

Have the children cut out paper figures for these felt boards and boxes. Provide bits of felt and glue to back the figures.

20. Make Finger Puppets to Use When Reading Special Poems or Stories

These puppets can be the heads of animals, the faces of children, vegetables with faces, toys, and so on.

Cardboard tubes from paper towels, waxed paper, or toilet paper can be used. Cloth tubes can also be made.

These tubes will fit the fingers of one or both hands. Attach heads to the tubes with glue, or attach small toys, animals, or objects.

21. Make Puppets on Sticks for Puppet Shows

Buy 3/8" dowel sticks at a paint or hardware store. Cut the sticks into suitable lengths to hold in the hands.

Use Play-Doh, clay, homemade dough, or Styrofoam to make the puppet heads. Shape, carve, and paint them with tempera, acrylic paint, or enamel. Add garments when needed.

Provide a small puppet stage. This can be made from a cardboard box, with an opening through which the puppets can perform.

After the puppets have been used by the teacher a number of times, her kindergartners will want to put on their own puppet shows. They probably will suggest other puppet characters they need. Make these additional characters as a class project.

Kindergartners are often very good at providing interesting dialogue for puppet shows. If possible record a few of these shows.

22. A Year-long Child-progress Activity

Start an I AM ＿＿ (child's name) project at the beginning of school, and continue it throughout the entire year.

Before school begins make enough folders for the entire anticipated enrollment. These folders should be made from 12" x 18" heavy white construction paper or oaktag. Fold the paper in half. Across the top print I AM ＿＿,leaving room for the child's name.

The first page of the child's book should be his or her self-portrait, made during the first week of school. This self-portrait may not be more than a few lines; it may be a head and mouth; the head may have stick legs. Whatever a child makes, that is the way he sees himself in his first week at school. (There will be other self-portraits in this book. The progress the child makes in manipulative skills, and in his changing self-concept, will be revealing, to the delight and amazement of his teacher and parents.)

The second page of the book must be supplied by his teacher. On it should be the date, the child's age, height, and weight. Below this information the teacher should make a tracing around the child's right hand.

MY FAMILY could be the title of the next page, the words put at the top of a 9" x 12" piece of construction paper. On this page the child should draw his father, mother, sisters and brothers, and a grandparent, if there is one in the home. A cat, dog, or other pet may have a prominent place on this family page. (It is not unlikely that some children will omit members of their homes in this first picture. The young child tends to ignore people or things that are not important to him, or are disliked by him.)

MY FAVORITE TOYS could title another page. This page should be done after the child has been in school awhile. On it he draws pictures of the toys he most enjoys playing with at home and at school.

I LIKE can title a page of pictured foods. These pictures can be cut from magazines or catalogs, or can be drawn by the children.

MY FRIENDS should title another page, with pictures drawn by the child; or he may choose to let his friends draw self-portraits on this page. The friends should also sign their pictures if they can print their names, for pictures drawn by very young artists are not always identifiable!

Pictured records of all school trips should be included in this book, as well as special days and events in the child's life. Some of these events may take place away from school. If children understand that they can contribute to their book at any time, they will feel free to make pictures and give them to their teacher to store in the book folder. They should be encouraged to contribute pages to their books that reflect their own individual interests, as well as group interests.

A page, or pages, should show newly learned skills, such as potato printing, finger painting, and so on. A flag, made by the child, properly displaying seven red stripes and six white ones, with a field of white stars should be included. The lines may be wobbly, and the stripes crooked, but making a picture of his own flag is an achievement of which the kindergartner is justifiably proud.

Neatly printed numerals or alphabet letters, a creative design using geometric shapes, or other creative designs of any nature should be included.

When kindergartners learn about the lives and habits of other peoples in the world, they like to draw pictures about them. These pictures can serve as records of interesting activities.

When the children have learned to print their own names, each child should have his friends' autographs on a page for his book.

The teacher's picture should be included. These pictures are usually surprising and always delightful! Beneath the child-drawn picture, the teacher should print her name.

Pictures of the child's home, church and the school are also good additions to the book.

About midyear another self-portrait should be drawn by the child, and again just before school ends. At midyear, and again just before term end, pages should be made as they were at the beginning of school, to record the child's weight, height, age, and the drawn outline of his right hand. He can then carefully outline his own hand.

One of the last pages in the book should show the child's fingerprints. These, he has learned, never change, however fast he grows.

Punch holes in the pages of each child's book, put on the cover, and tie the book together with string or bright yarn. Before the string is tied, let each child put reinforcements on the punched holes so the pages will not tear.

Each kindergartner can be very proud of his or her own school "story" told in pictures. Children will look at the pages many times and discuss the pictured events with their classmates.

Most parents are delighted and grateful to have this pictured progress report made by their child.

Display Areas

Place an upright piano at a right angle to the wall, its back visible to the work and play areas in the kindergarten room. Use the back of the piano for a display area.

Coverings for the Piano Back

23. Corrugated Paper

Cover the piano back with one large sheet of corrugated paper, or fasten several smaller pieces together with masking tape to cover the piano back. Cover the entire paper cover with felt. This makes a display area within easy reach of young children. It can be used for felt-board number games, visual perception games, story demonstrations with felt figures, and many other games.

24. Pegboard

Put a permanent back on the piano with pegboard. This will have to be done by someone other than the teacher, of course. Buy various hooks for use on this pegboard. Small shelves for storage can be put up, and innumerable objects can be displayed there, all within easy reach of small children.

25. Cork

A permanent cork backing can be put on the piano back. Papers, pictures, bulletin-board materials, a calendar, and so on, can all be thumbtacked to the cork covering.

26. Muslin

Use the piano back to permanently display special drawings kindergartners have made while working on a science, nature, citizenship, or other activity.

Buy a piece of unbleached muslin large enough to cover the piano back. Hem the material or bind the edges with bias tape.

When pictures have been selected for reproduction on this cloth, the teacher should show the kindergartner the spot on the cloth where he is to redraw his special picture. Each picture should have color applied thickly, so there is built-up crayon on every line and on every colored area in the picture.

After all pictures have been redrawn on the cloth, the teacher should cover a flat surface with brown paper. The cloth is put on the brown paper *crayon side down*. Dip a soft piece of cloth (an old sheet will do) in vinegar. Cover one area at a time and press the cloth with an iron. The heat regulator should be set at *cotton*. Keep the pressing cloth damp with vinegar, and press the entire cloth. The hot iron melts the crayon and the vinegar in the pressing cloth sets the color in the cloth.

Turn the cloth over. There, in permanent color, is a record of children's art. This cloth can be washed in cold water without affecting the color.

Attach the decorative cloth to the piano back. Kindergartners are proud of it as a record of an enjoyable activity.

Make a new cloth covering as each new group of kindergartners comes along. The old coverings can be used as wall hangings, to make a frieze for a hall decoration, or in other suggested ways. Some kindergarten groups may want the covering to accompany the class to the new room they will occupy the next year.

27. Folding Screen

An old folding screen can be covered with burlap, felt, or heavy paper. This makes an effective display area for papers, children's hand-crafted objects, and so on.

28. Window Shades

If floor space is limited in the classroom and the teacher needs display areas or teaching charts, use heavy white window shades. A custodian can put the shade brackets above the chalkboard or other display areas that are in constant use, and the shades can be pulled down, used, and then rolled back.

Buy several shades for different uses. Charts for daily or infrequent use can be done with felt-tipped pens. On other shades pictures can be displayed. The rolled-up chart can be lifted out of the shade bracket and another one can replace it.

Shades used in this way have many advantages. They take up very little space when taken down and stored. They can be pulled down within the reach of small children. They may cover another permanent display area, but they can be removed in a few minutes.

Display and Storage

29. Orange Crates

Use wooden orange crates or apple boxes for display and storage. These boxes can be obtained at fruit and vegetable stores, and cost very little. Sometimes they are freely given to a teacher by the merchant.

Glue, nail, or tie these crates together with cord. Paint them with enamel in gay colors. Use them for bookcases, or as storage for art materials, toys, children's folders, and so on. Use them for special projects, or as a store or pet shop. Attach paper slats to the open fronts of these boxes, and use them as animal cages for zoo or circus projects.

These boxes can be used singly as storage boxes for toys or blocks. Paint them in gay colors, and decorate them with geometric or other designs in contrasting colors. Have ball-bearing casters put on the four corners of the boxes. They can then be rolled from place to place in the classroom.

With wheels attached, these boxes make excellent train cars when kindergartners are learning about transportation. An engine can be made by using smaller paper boxes fastened to the larger wooden one. Other wooden boxes serve as various train cars. They can be tied together and pushed (very slowly!) around the room.

30. Cardboard Boxes

Use heavy cardboard boxes for display and storage. Fasten them together with glue or *very* long paper fasteners. Paint the boxes and use them for displaying and storing lightweight objects. Use them for doll houses or toy shops.

31. Box-stacks

Fasten various sizes of cardboard boxes together with

one large box at the bottom for a sturdy base. All four sides of each box should be closed before it is fastened to other boxes.

Stack one box on top of another using glue, very long paper fasteners, or masking tape to fasten the boxes together.

This tall box-stack can be used in many ways. It can be painted by children as a totem pole. It can be painted in many colors with poster paints, then used to display pictures or other objects. Children can paint pictures directly on the cardboard.

The box-stack can be used as a "tree" for imaginative play.

chapter two

19 Activities That Teach Word Sounds and Good Listening Habits

Introducing the Sounds of Letters

1. Display the Alphabet

The alphabet should be displayed on the child's eye level, if possible.

Introduce the sounds of the alphabet letters, one at a time. Explain that each letter in the alphabet says its own name. The children will learn each name and letter sound. Later on they may learn at least one more sound of most of the letters.

2. Learning to Make Sounds

Preparation: Make 3" x 4" cards of cardboard or oaktag. On each card print an alphabet letter with which the childrens' names begin.

Make a large chart with a column of pictures at the left. These pictures may be drawn by the teacher, or cut from magazines. They should show (1) a face, (2) open lips and teeth, (3) closed lips, (4) a face, neck, and chest, (5) an open mouth with the tongue showing between the teeth, and (6) a face with a prominent nose.

Use this chart to explain that the lips, teeth, and tongue are used most in shaping some letter sounds. To make other letter sounds, *H,* for example, a child must use his breath. The sound of *M* is a sound made with the lips and throat, and seems to be pushed out through the nose.

Ask the children to try the sound of *A.* Were the lips and

teeth used in making the sound of *A?* Did the sound come up out of the throat? When the children have decided the answers to these questions, put an *A* beside the correct picture on the chart. Indicate, with a circle around the pictured area, just what they think helped to make the *A* sound.

Talk about only a few sounds each day, so the children can thoroughly learn each one. Continue until all the letters of the alphabet have been experimented with and learned.

Talk about the ways in which the sounds are made. Is the breath pushed out, or sucked in to make certain sounds? How does the sound *feel* in the child's mouth and throat? Does the sound come out easily? Does it tickle a bit? If a child has front teeth missing, can he still make some of the sounds?

Encourage children to experiment with sounds. Which of the alphabet letter sounds do they most enjoy making? Which letters are the hardest for them to make?

Play These Games

(1) Spread 3" x 4" alphabet cards on a table. Give each child in the class his own name card. (These first-name cards should be part of the classroom's teaching aids.) Call the class roll. As each child's name is called, he comes to the table and finds the letter with which his name begins. He shows it, with his name, to the teacher and class, and gives the sound of the the letter. He then returns the letter to the table.

(2) The teacher divides the class into several groups, with one child as "leader" of each group. The teacher holds up a letter and the first group must give the name sound of the letter, and one other sound if they have learned it, as *A* in "aim" and *A* as in "apple." The group of children should then try to think of familiar words that begin with both sounds of *A.* "Amy," "as," "apple" are some that may be named. The word "aigs," for "eggs" is invariably chosen for one of the sounds!

Continue the game with new groups and new letter sounds. Each group should have turns at sounding several letters, and at finding words that begin with that sound. The letters *U, X,* and *Z* should not be used in this game. Explain that the children would know few words with those beginning sounds.

3. My Own Name

Preparation: The teacher should use 12" x 18" construction paper. (Larger paper should be used for very long names.)

On each sheet print a child's name, leaving plenty of space between each letter. Draw parallel lines between each letter. Show these sheets to the children, and explain that *all* the letters in a child's name, when sounded together, make a particular sound, as in "David," "Susan," "Judy," or "Brian."

Print the word SUSAN on the board. Draw parallel lines between each letter. Explain and demonstrate how each letter in a name also has its own special sound. Ask someone to think of an object whose name begins with *S.* "Stone" and "snake" are suggested. The teacher makes small sketches of a stone and a snake beneath the letter *S.*

Ask for familiar words beginning with the *uh* sound of *U.* "Umbrella" and "uncle" are mentioned. Sketch an umbrella and a small stick man beneath the letter *U.* Continue with the other letters until SUSAN has objects beneath each letter.

Show the children their own name papers again and explain that each name may be taken home by its owner. At home the child can look through magazines, old catalogs, or newspapers and cut out pictures of objects with names that begin with the letters in the child's own name. These cut-out pictures should be brought to school in an envelope, along with the name sheet.

At school the child can paste each pictured object under the correct letter-sound in his name. (If a child cannot find pictures at home, supply him with old magazines at school. Encourage those children who can draw to illustrate their sheets with their own drawings.)

Kindergartners enjoy the very personal participation in this game. They are proud to see their MY OWN NAME sheets displayed in the room.

4. Letter-sounds and Pictures

This game is played to help children recognize the beginning letter sounds in their names. Ask a child whose name begins with *C* (as Cathy, Carl, or Carol) to name an animal whose name *also* begins with *C.* If "cat" is chosen, explain that a cat picture is to be drawn on the board, or on an easel. The cat picture will not be drawn by one child, however, but by several children whose names begin with the first letters of certain parts of a cat. Does any child have a name beginning with *B?* He may use chalk (or crayon) to make the body of a cat. A child whose name begins with *H* may make the head of the cat. Continue with various parts of the animal's body until the cat picture has been finished. So that more children can be involved ask for suggestions about things to add to the cat's picture, such as a "bow" around its neck, with a "bell" on it, "spots" on its fur, "claws" on its toes, and so on. Allow the children to be imaginative as they think of ways to add to the picture.

Some children in the room may have names beginning with letters that cannot fit into a picture of any kind. Those children can choose a beginning letter-sound by saying, "My name starts with____," so they, too, may draw part of a picture.

Note: As this game is played, the teacher should direct the choice of objects toward those that lend themselves to being decorated or added to in many ways. A train, suggested by a child whose name begins with *T,* is an excellent object to draw, with its engine, cow-catcher, whistle, bell, wheels, rails, tender, hopper, cattlecar, refrigerator car, boxcar, piggy-back car, flat car, tankcr, and caboose. Many children could participate in this drawing.

5. Rhymes and Riddles, with Sounds and Words

Read these nonsense rhymes to kindergartners, and encourage them to make up their own rhymes with sounds and words.

> I like chicken,
>   I like cheese.
> I *don't* like pepper.
>   It makes me sneeze.

> From a tree
>   I pick cherries.

From a bush
   I pick berries.
Did you know a mouse
   Lives in our house?
We will get a cat
   To take care of *that!*
Little Johnnie Jensen
   Ran away toward town.
Bouncing his ball
   Up and down.
A cross old Billy goat
   Chased Johnnie home.
Now he tells me
   He is afraid to roam.
B and *V* sound the same,
   Velvet and *vest* begin with *V*
But *B* begins both *boy* and *Bruce,*
   And Bruce is my name!

Ask the children a few riddles. The first three use words with a *ch* sound.

What is made from sour milk?   (cheese)
What grows on a tree?   (cherries)
What hangs around a girl's neck and has a locket on it?   (chain)
What *r*uns but has no legs?   (river)
I am thinking of one big thing and one little animal whose names rhyme, but *do not* start with the same sounds. What are they?   (house and mouse)

Encourage the children to think of riddles using beginning sounds. Use the best ones and display them on a bulletin board.

6. Silly Sounds

Young children enjoy hearing and making gay, silly, rollicking sounds that are not real words.

Ask kindergartners this question, "How does a train sound as it travels along its tracks?" The answers they will give are unusual. The trains sounds clackity, bumbly; it clicks and bings and bangs; it clunks and chunks; it whoos and woos and screeches and meeches.

If the kindergarten group is made up of children who may never have heard a train, choose some noisy household appliance, like an electric sweeper, or some often-heard object like an airplane or tractor, and let the children express their ideas of the noises made by the object. What noises are made by the huge construction machines on the city street corner?

Children will say that whistles scream, gream, chill, scrill, woo-woo, hoo-hoo, and in the house the doorbell goes ringity, rangity, plealing, screaling.

When Mother fries food in a hot skillet the grease goes sizzily, sazzily, frizzily, frazzily, sizzling, bizzling, poppity, stoppity.

Guide the children to express themselves in many sound combinations of silly words. Encourage them to make up stories using their nonsense words.

Ask some children to make up silly words about a favorite toy or pet. This is an excellent way to get shy children to express themselves, and talk to their classmates.

Ask the kindergartners to say some silly sounds with you, like dissity, dossity; alunk, kerplunk; plickety, plackity. How do these words feel in their mouths when children say them? Are the lips, tongue, teeth, and breath *all* used in sounding the words? Do these silly sounds make the children think of any particular animal that might make them?

Can the children say such words as tissity, tassity, and sillity, sollity with the teeth held tightly together?

Words like whirring, purring, or hillity, hollity require lots of breath to make them. Can the children say these word-sounds with their lips tightly closed?

As they experiment with sounds the children will become more aware of the way in which lips, teeth, tongue, throat, and breath all help in making sounds.

The following are nonsense words kindergartners will love:

plickity, plackity	ziggily, zaggily
quillity, quality	yimminy, yamminy
willity, wollity	screechable, meechable
hippity, hoppity	skittering, flittering
skillity, scollity	nissity, nassity

rillity, rollity

millity, mollity

jillity, jollity

tamminy, tomminy

hammering, yammering

skirring, whirring

mickity, mockity

nickity, nockity

splitikey, splotikey

rustico, bustico

billico, bollico

billity, bollity

beasties, feasties

chillies, quillies

dissity, dossity

hickety, hackety

clickity, clackity

rickity, rackity

himiny, hominy

sillico, sollico

tissity, tassity

tillity, tollity

7. What Do I Say?

Preparation: Make picture cards of animals with which children are familiar. Display the alphabet at the child's eye level, if possible.

Show the picture cards to the class, one at a time. Identify the animals and discuss the sound (or sounds) each one makes.

The lion roars. Ask some child to use a pointer and point to the alphabet letter with which the word "roar" begins, the *r-r* sound. Ask another child to point to the beginning letter of the *oink* sound a pig makes. What sound does a rooster make, and what is the beginning letter-sound of his crow?

After discussing several animals and the sounds made by them, the children are ready for the *What Do I Say?* cards. A child is given an animal card by the teacher. He makes the sound the pictured animal would make. He then points to the alphabet letter that begins the name of the animal. If his classmates agree that he has pointed to the correct letter, and has made the correct sound, he may choose a picture card, call a classmate's name and ask "What Do I Say?" The game continues until all the children have had a turn.

The teacher may want to continue further with this game and put the names of the sounds on the board or on a chart, such as meow, baa, oink, hee-haw, bark, neigh or whinny, howl, crow or cock-a-doodle-do, cluck, honk, roar and hiss. Place the animal cards on a table. Help the children identify the names of the sounds, and have the children discuss the beginning letters of the sound names. Next, hold up the animal cards and help the children match the animal picture to the sound it makes. Some children can identify the sound-names by their beginning letters. They may then choose the picture of the animal that makes a particular sound.

8. Let's Play Detective

Preparation: Provide a number of cards with the names of objects familiar to children printed on them, such as boat, boy, girl, bicycle, bell, car, cat, dog, doll, top, table, mittens, mouse, and so on.

Display these cards along a chalk tray, or in a place where they can be easily seen by all the children.

Explain the game. Detectives solve all kinds of problems by finding *clues* that tell them things about what has happened. The teacher will give the children some clues, or hints, so they may easily guess the object she has chosen to talk about.

First Clue: The beginning sound in the name is buh. Ask one child to collect all the words that begin with *B,* or the *buh* sound, and display them together.

Second Clue: The object helps people to get from place to place. The name of the object has four letters in it. (At this point a child might choose the word "boat," or the word "bell.") If no correct answer is given, continue with another hint.

Third Clue: The name of this object begins with the sound of buh *and the last letter of the word is* T.

When a child guesses the correct word from the clue given, he must show the card to the class. He should say the name of the object, "boat." He names each letter in the word.

After playing this game with names of familiar objects, let the children give the clues. The teacher will tell the child what the word says, so he may think of good hints or clues. Shy children or slow learners, when they have been told the word, are often surprisingly good at thinking of good clues. It helps them to express themselves in sentences. They have something important to talk about, which builds self-esteem.

Playing this game stimulates the desire to read. After playing it together in class, children will ask to play it in their free time together. Many kindergartners soon recognize all the words on the cards. They can easily relate them to the objects they name.

9. Sound of the Month

It is not too early to begin in September with this game of *Sound of the Month.* Although kindergartners are in school for the first time (unless they have attended nursery school), they will find the sound of *S* easy to make. Ask them to think of a word that begins with the *s-s-s* sound. They may think of a number of words, such as see, start, stone, syrup, sausage, store, sneak, silly, Sam, sound, snake, Susan, Sarah, sorry, swing, song, sing, sister, sizzle, supper, sit, sat, stand, small, sometimes, sent, several, skip, skate, squirrel, scissors, story, said. If the children are slow in thinking of words, the teacher can suggest a few to stimulate their thinking.

The game is played with the children standing in a circle. Before the game begins, the teacher should review all the words the children have given her. Pronounce them with the children. Explain that these words beginning with the *s-s-s* sound will be used in the game.

Ask the first child to give a word that starts with the *s-s-s* sound. If he cannot think of one, he may ask the child on each side of him in the circle. If all *three* cannot think of a word, the first child must sit on the floor. He is out of the game. Continue around the circle until each child has had a turn. The teacher should decide how many times a word can be used.

Play another game to encourage listening for words and sounds. Make up an amusing story, using many words that begin with *S;* or tell a sad story. Read or tell it to the class one or more times, making the words beginning with *S* quite loud and outstanding, so the children will remember them.

Explain to the children that the story will be read, or told again. This time, when they hear a word that begins with the *s-s-s* sound, they should raise their hands. The teacher should stop now and then and ask the children to say the words they hear, or pause after a paragraph and ask to have *all* the words repeated. This will encourage careful listening. Kindergartners love this kind of supply-the-word game.

A Sample Story

Two *sisters,* whose names were *Sarah* and *Susan,* were *skating* home from the *store.* Their mother had *sent* them to the *store* to buy *some syrup* and *sausage.* *She* wanted to *serve* pancakes and *sausage* for their *supper.*

Suddenly Susan stopped and *said,* "Oh, *Sarah!* I *see* a *slimly snake* there by the *sidewalk!* I will throw a *stone* at it!"

Her big *sister Sarah said,* "*Shame* on you! Don't be *silly, Susan.* You can *see* that *snake* is too *small* to hurt you. Besides, it is a harmless *snake.*"

"I'm *sorry,*" said Susan.

They *saw* the *small snake slowly slither* away.

Susan started to *sing.* "*Slimy snake,* why do you hiss?" "*S-s-s-ss,*" he *said.* "I talk like this."

She said to *Sarah,* "I'm glad you *stopped* me. You *saved* that *small snake's* life."

Vary the Sound-of-the-Month game by asking questions or making statements with blanks left in them so kindergartners can supply the words. Read these to them several times with the words in them before asking the children to supply the missing words.

Some examples for January:

Is this orange *juice* for me?

Bobby, will you please hang up your *jacket*?

Most children like to run and *jump* when they play.

A *jolly* Santa says "Ho-ho-ho!"

If you have several pennies in your pocket, you can *jingle* them.

I asked my mother to spread *jam* on my slice of bread.

I like peanut butter and *jelly* sandwiches.

Last summer I caught fireflies and put them in a *jar.*

Encourage kindergartners to make up stories, questions, or sentences in which there are many words with the sound-of-the-month.

10. Sounds of the Seasons

Children hear sounds they learn to "tune out." They become oblivious to the sounds around them. The following activities will help kindergartners to become more aware of sounds and eager to identify them. They will associate sounds with the living creatures that make them, or with machines. These activities will help children understand the ways in which people are affected by sounds.

These activities are designed for both the city child and the country child. Most city children have never visited the country and some have very little knowledge of country life, while most country children have visited small towns and know very little about the city. When teachers read stories and show pictures of both city and country life, kindergartners begin to understand another way of life different from their own. There are new and exciting sounds they may never have heard.

Sounds in the City

How conscious are city children of the sounds around them? "Can anyone in the room imitate the sound of a fire siren?" "Does an ambulance siren sound just like a fire siren?" "How does a big bus sound when it pulls away from the curb?" "When it pulls up at the corner to let passengers out does it make a different kind of sound?"

Does a factory whistle blow near the home of any child in the room? At what time of day does it blow? Is it before breakfast, or after breakfast? Is it at noon, or at night? Is there a large clock that chimes the hour?

"What are the sounds the newsboy makes at the corner newsstand?" "Does he say real words or does he just make sounds?" "What does he say?"

"Who hears large construction machines?" "Where are the machines?" "What kinds of sounds do they make?" "What kinds of work are the machines doing?" "Do the sounds change or are they always the same?"

How many children must pass noisy buildings on their way to school? Does the noise in the building come from machines? Can the children hear the voices of people who run the machines?

Is there a railroad track near the homes of children in the room? Do they cross the railroad tracks on their way to school?

Is there a flasher signal at the crossing? Does it make a noise? What is the sound of the warning signal?

"What are some kinds of transportation in the city?" "What sounds do they make?"

"Are there sounds in the city that are heard *only* on Sundays?" "How do church bells sound?"

Discuss all these sounds and any others the children may mention. Ask kindergartners to look in newspapers and magazines for pictures of city sound-makers. Use these pictures to make a bulletin board of city sounds.

Which of the city sounds they hear are pleasant sounds? Are there any sounds that frighten them? When they hear certain sounds, does it mean that something exciting is about to happen? Are there sounds that make them sad? Encourage the children to talk freely about the ways in which they are affected by sounds.

Are city sounds in the night louder or more disturbing (or scary) than the same sounds heard in the daytime? This talk about ways in which children react to sounds may reveal fears and frustrations. Through such discussions a teacher may better understand a troubled child's behavior at school.

Make a List of City Sounds of the Seasons

Many sounds are heard throughout the entire year, such as church bells, fire sirens, ambulance sirens, sounds of transportation, and so on.

The thunder of snowplows, the scrape of snow shovels, the squeak of snow under the feet on a cold day, and wind whistling around windows and rattling doors are all sounds heard only in winter.

Sounds of big construction machines, street sprinklers, lawnmowers, and the buzzing of insects are all sounds of spring and summer.

"Do city birds, such as pigeons, starlings, and sparrows, chirp or coo all year?" "Are birds heard more often in one season than another?" "Are city birds heard in the winter?"

Make a Sounds of the Seasons bulletin board.

Sounds in the Country

The city teacher will need to read many stories about the country and its ways, and show many pictures and filmstrips to city children to familiarize them with the country and its sounds.

Country sounds are more seasonal than city sounds. Birds sing in their nesting period. For some birds this may happen only in the spring. Other birds may raise more than one family, so their songs are heard in the summer.

Spring in the country is the season when the "peepers" begin to sing. The voices of other frogs are heard later in the spring and on summer evenings. Baby animals are born, and baby farmyard fowl are hatched in the spring. Their baby voices are all part of the sound of spring in the country, and their adult voices can be heard during the other seasons.

The steady noise of tractors in the fields is something the country child may learn to ignore, just as he ignores the sound of buzzsaws and other power tools as farmers go about their work. These sounds are distinctive and interesting. Discussion of them will make the country child aware of them in relation to the various machines necessary to present-day work on farms. Harvesting machines make up the sounds of country life in the summer and fall.

How many insects can country children identify by their sounds? Discuss insects and the ways in which they make sounds. Are all insect sounds pleasant to hear? (See chapter 7 on nature.)

Encourage the children to freely express themselves about the sounds they hear. Are they frightened at the hooting of an owl? Do certain sounds they hear tell them that certain events will soon take place?

Remind kindergartners to be aware of each *new* and unfamiliar sound they hear, and encourage them to investigate the source of new sounds. "Did a door slam somewhere? Why?" "Is that a cricket under the log?" "Could that faint, mewing sound be new kittens in the hayloft?" "Why are the chickens in the henhouse making such a racket?" "Where is that screech owl whose plaintive cry keeps a child from going to sleep?" "Is that the whimper of a stray puppy? Is it under the porch?" "Are those darting birds above that building making that strange, sad cry?"

Children should listen for sounds on their way to school. They will enjoy sharing each new sound experience with their classmates.

11. Listening for Beginning Sounds, or What Is the Right Word?

The teacher should explain that she will read some interesting statements or questions to the children. In these there will be one word whose beginning sound the teacher will make. There will be another word in the statement that begins with the same sound. The children are to listen carefully so they can supply the missing word.

For example: The teacher says, "Here is a *buh-button.* Please put it in a _____ on the table." (The children should supply the word "box.")

When the children understand the game, use these statements:

1. A pretty *puh-picture* is hanging above the _____. [piano]
2. Here is a *buh-bunch* of _____. [bananas]
3. My *tuh-turtle* swims in a _____ of water. [tub]
4. Put this bread in the *tuh-toaster* on the _____. [table]
5. That *luh-lamp* gives a bright _____. [light]
6. I have two things to write with, a *puh-pen* and a _____. [pencil]
7. This is *cuh-cold cuh-coffee* in my _____. [cup]
8. Do you like *cuh-candy, cuh-cake* and _____? [cookies]
9. This *shuh-shirt* has _____ sleeves. [short]
10. A garden *huh-hose* is _____ inside. [hollow]
11. A *cuh-can* opener _____ the can lid. [cuts]
12. I like all kinds of candy, but my *chuh-choice* is _____. [chocolate]

12. Listening and Identifying Sounds

Divide the class into small groups. Each group should choose someone to act as spokesman.

Explain that sounds will be made by the teacher, one at a time. These sounds will be made with familiar objects such as, two erasers clapped together, a chair pulled across the floor, scissors dropped from a table, a note played on the piano, a ticking alarm clock, a window being closed or opened, the slam of a door, and so on.

The children must close their eyes at a signal. They will listen to the sound made by the teacher. They may open their eyes at a signal. The children in each group discuss the sound and tell their spokesman what they think it was. The spokesman raises his hand and the teacher records the decision of each group.

After the children have listened to all the sounds, identified them, and the spokesman has reported, the teacher will check the scores of each group. The group that has recognized the most sounds will win.

13. High and Low Sounds

This is an activity of listening for high sounds and low sounds. The teacher plays notes on the piano, sings bars of music, hums tunes, uses bells, taps on water glasses or on china dishes, lets the air out of balloons of various sizes, and makes noises with any object that will produce distinctly high or low sounds.

The listening is done as a group. The children raise their arms high above their heads when they hear high sounds. If there are individuals who seem confused and cannot make a choice between high and low sounds, the teacher can make a note to have the child's hearing checked.

14. Identification and Association of Sounds
with Words and Objects

Begin this game by asking kindergartners what sound they think of when they think of a *bee*. Some may answer "b-z-z-z." "Does the word 'buzz' begin with the same sound that 'bee' begins with?"

"What kind of a sound does a *snake* make?" The answer is usually "s-s-s-s." Some child will say, "That's the same sound *snake* starts with." Another child may have discovered that the words "snake" and "make" rhyme; while still another may say, "Yes, but my *cat* goes s-s-s-s at our dog and *cat* doesn't start with an s-s-s-s sound."

Ask children to make insect sounds or animal sounds, and let their classmates decide whether the beginning sounds are the same as the names of the creatures that made them.

Talk about machines. Many children love to imitate sounds machines make. Cars, trains, and buses when they come to a corner and stop, or merely slow down, make noises that children love to imitate. Large construction machines, and all kinds of aircraft make noises with which children are familiar. Ask the children to reproduce some of these sounds. Associate the sounds with the sounds of letters. Encourage them to enunciate each sound carefully, especially those that sound much alike such as *m* and *n, b* and *v, g* and *j,* and point out that the letters *c* and *k* often have the same sounds.

Make sure that each child in the room participates in this identification and association of sounds activity. Spend extra time with the slow learner. Through his own contributions, the letters he sees and the sounds he has been trying to learn suddenly make sense to him. The teacher helps him to discover that his kitten says "meow," and it drinks milk; and both words start with an *m-m-m* sound! He knows the m-m-m sound, for he often hums it when the rest of the children in the room are singing songs and saying words!

Children make sounds from babyhood—sounds that comfort them, sounds that delight them. In kindergarten these sounds gain new meaning.

15. Listening for Rhyming Words

Preparation: Explain that the children will be asked to listen carefully to some rhymes. Each rhyme has two or more rhyming words in it. Ask the children to put their heads on their desks or tables. They must close their eyes while they listen to the first rhyme. When it is finished they may raise their hands. When called upon, a child must repeat *all* the rhyming words he heard.

1. What is a coat?
   What is a goat?
   What is a submarine?
   What is a boat?

If the first child called on cannot give *all* the rhyming words, call on another child for the remaining words.

2. What is a tank?
   What is a bank?
   When you receive a present
   Whom do you thank?
3. What is a scar?
   What is tar?
   I collect lightning bugs
   In a jar.
4. What is sap?
   What is a scrap?
   Water in the bathroom
   Runs out of a tap.
5. What is a shield?
   What is a field?
   When you say "Give up!"
   Do you yield?
6. In our house
   Is a mouse.
   He eats our rice.
   That isn't nice.
7. What is money?
   What is honey?
   What big, round object
   Makes our days sunny?
8. Our cat and dog
   Are not alike.
   The cat's name is Smog.
   The dog's name is Mike.

Ask the children to make up their own nonsense rhymes. Also, read poetry to the children, and ask them to listen for rhyming words.

16. Listening for Story Details

Read a familiar story to the class. Ask the children to put their heads down and close their eyes. Reread the story, changing some important details.

Question the kindergartners about the story. Was it exactly the same story they heard the first time? Did it sound almost the same? What was wrong in the second story? Was the house in the city? In the woods? What were the colors of the boy's clothes?

If nobody discovered the mistakes, read the story once more, changing it in more details until the children can find the errors.

Listening for story meaning. Remind children to listen very carefully to a new story. Choose a very short story with many time or place details.

When the story is finished, question the children for details about it to check how carefully they listen for meaning.

17. What Is Its Name?

Listening to familiar songs. The teacher chooses songs that are familiar to the class. She may either hum a few bars of the song, sing a verse of a song, or play part of the song on the piano while the children listen.

The children are to raise their hands as soon as they recognize the name of the song. Be sure to observe those children who never recognize *any* tune.

18. A Telephone Game

Use play telephones or telephones cut from cardboard or oaktag for this game.

The teacher makes the first telephone call to one of the children. She gives him some information. He must listen, then repeat *all* the information to the class.

All the children have listened to the teacher's call, and they have heard what the child repeated. They must decide whether the child heard *all* of the information, *part* of the information, or *very little* of it.

The teacher makes a listening chart on the board. Draw three columns and write at the top ALL, MOST, VERY LITTLE. Write each child's name and check his listening score with an x in the proper column.

As the teacher continues the telephone calls, so each child may have a turn, she can use many details that will interest the entire class, such as, "The Brown family has a new puppy. It is white, with black ears and tail." "There is a tall white church on Main Street. Pigeons live in the belfry of the church." "Today I saw a firetruck going to a fire. A spotted dog rode on the truck." "The bakery sells cookies, pies, cakes and bread."

19. Private-eye Clues, or Three Guesses

Preparation: Make cards with pictures of familiar objects and their printed names. The names of the objects should be short, and their beginning letters should include as many alphabet letters as possible. Suggested objects are: boat, bed, box, car, cat, table, wagon, bike, top, dog, mittens, shoes, house, jar, goat, and mouse.

The teacher begins the game with the first clue, so the children may make a first guess. She does *not* show the object card.

1st clue—This object's name begins with "b." The object can be big or little.

2nd clue—It helps people to get from place to place. What is it? [If nobody guesses "boat" the 3rd clue is given.]

3rd clue—It can be run with a motor or oars. What is it?

The first child to guess the word may come up to the teacher, hold up the boat card and point to the name. If he likes, he can say the names of the letters in the word "boat." He then gets to select a picture (without showing it to the class) and he will give three clues to its name.

If there are shy children or slow learners in the class, let them choose a partner, which will give them more confidence and help them make some correct guesses. The partners can then work together to think of clues.

chapter three

14 Games and Activities That Improve Word Understanding and Vocabulary

1. A Game of Opposites

Preparation: Talk with the class about words that are *opposite* to each other, such as *up* and *down, in* and *out, big* and *little.* Let the children freely discuss these and other word opposites they mention.

Use the following list and introduce one word of a combination, asking the children to furnish its opposite. Going through the list delete words that seem too difficult for the group to comprehend. Add words the children have contributed to the list.

front—back	tall—short
give—take	fat—skinny, lean
to—from	soft—hard
go—come	wet—dry
there—here	ugly—pretty
high—low	long—short
big—little	none—many
hot—cold	more—less
large—small	cloudy—sunny
tiny—huge, big	wet—dry
noise—quiet, silence	frown—smile
dim—bright	cry—laugh
happy—sad, glad	up—down
in—out	heavy—light
south—north	light—dark
east—west	queen—king
right—left	prince—princess

winter—summer	dwarf—giant
fall—spring	boy—girl
far—near	man—woman
true—false, not true	good—bad

The game: Discuss the list, or part of the list. Ask children to sit in a circle. The teacher gives a child one word, and he must give its opposite. If he cannot think of its opposite, he may ask for help from a classmate. If neither child knows the answer, the first one must sit outside the circle. (The only way he may reenter the game is to be asked to supply a word for another player and know the word.)

Continue to give words around the circle until each child in the class has had a turn.

Children love this game and will play it often. Soon there will be *no* children sitting outside the circle.

2. Hand-Foot Game (a riddle and question game)

This game, when introduced, is always a surprise to children, who assume it will be a physical game played with the hands and feet.

The teacher begins the game by asking if *anyone knows what handcuffs are.* The question brings a lot of response. She points out that the word "handcuffs" has the word "hand" in it, and almost *tells* what it means.

b. *The second question:* Something in this room besides you boys, girls and your teacher, has hands. What is it? [clock]

c. Why are the two pointers on the clock called *hands*? Are *our* hands ever used as pointers? How?

d. *Give this riddle next*: What has the word "hand" in it, but is used on the nose? [handkerchief]

e. *Another riddle:* What has the word "hand" in it and might be seen on the chalkboard or on paper? [handwriting]

f. If a lady knits a pretty sweater, or makes a pretty decoration for her house, the things she makes are_____, a word with "hand" in it. What is the word? [handmade]

g. The word "foot" is a part of many words, too. Who can think of the name of a game that has the word "foot" in it? [football] How do you think it got its name?

  h. If you walked on Mother's clean floor you might leave a
     dirty_____. [footprint]
  i. The word "footwear" is another name for shoes. Do you know
     why? Can you think of other kinds of footwear?
  j. What is the name of a small bridge used by people to cross a
     stream or a deep canyon? [footbridge]
  k. A little path to walk on through the woods or fields might be
     called a_____? [footpath]
  l. *Another riddle:* What sits on the floor and has a name that begins
     with "foot"? [footstool]

Children will want to make up questions or riddles of their own
to ask their classmates and their teacher. Encourage them to
bring ideas from home if they like.

A *Hand* and *Foot* Story

[Before the teacher begins the story, she reminds the
children to listen carefully, for there will be many hand and
foot words in the story. When it is finished, she asks them to
tell her as many words as they can recall.]

One dark night Tom Tanner, who was a well-known
policeman, was going home. He had to cross Pebble Creek on a
footbridge, then walk along a narrow *footpath* through a
woods. This woods was at the *foot* of a mountain.

Suddenly he heard a sound behind him in the darkness. Was
it the *footfall* of someone following him?

Tom stopped and listened. The sound came again, the
sound of stealthy *footsteps* on the *footpath* behind him. He
turned suddenly and crashed into a man.

They struggled together in the darkness but Policeman Tom
Tanner was very strong and well-trained. He fastened *handcuffs* on the man's *hands* as he lay there on the *footpath.* Then
he pulled the man to his *feet* and flashed a light into his face.
It was Foxy the *Footpad,* a famous, hard-to-catch robber.

"Get going!" Policeman Tom Tanner told his captive. He
followed *Footpad* back along the *footpath* and across the
footbridge to the police station.

3. Find Your Partners (a dramatization game of belong-together characters)

Use this list of story characters that belong together.

Hansel and Gretel
Gingerbread Man—farmers, animals
Jack and Jill
Jack-Be-Nimble—candlestick
Old King Cole—pipe, bowl, fiddlers three
Owl—Pussycat, pea-green boat
Three Billy Goats Gruff—Troll
Little Red Riding Hood—Wolf, grandmother, woodsman
Goldilocks—Three bears
Jack and the Beanstalk—Giant
Snow White—seven dwarfs
Pinocchio—old man
Ugly Duckling—animals
[add other storybook characters with which the class is familiar]

Assign names of characters to children. By naming all the dwarfs and the animals in the Ugly Duckling story, and so on, there will be enough characters so each child in the class may play. On a piece of paper jot down the child's name beside the name of the story character assigned to him, to avoid confusion later on.

When all the characters have been assigned, the teacher says, "When I call the name of a story, all the children who have parts in that story *must find their partners.* Children in a particular story should stand together until all children have found their partners." (Somebody always forgets who he is and where he belongs, so the teacher can check her list and find his group for him.)

Dramatizations come next, and all groups will not have time to "play" their parts in the stories unless this game is continued from day to day. The children will enjoy talking over their parts and preparing their stories. Some will want to make hats or simple costumes to wear.

This role-playing is an excellent learning experience for slow learners or shy or withdrawn children. They learn to associate stories with their characters, learn new vocabulary words, and enjoy the group participation in this activity. They often learn to speak with confidence before their classmates in this imaginative play.

4. What Do You Think Of?
(a game with body words)

Begin the game with a question like this: "What do you think of when you hear the word 'head'?" [hair, hat, headband, face]

Explain that this game *What Do You Think Of?* can be played *only* with names of parts of our bodies, such as hands, feet, mouth, teeth, ears, fingers, toes, nails, shoulder, arm, knee, heel, nose, eyes, leg, arm, hair, head, chin, waist, skin, and so on.

Children come to the front of the group, one at a time, and mention a part of the body. The child's classmates will then give the word associations. (The teacher may want to make notes of some of the answers given, for word associations often reveal much about the child who makes them.)

Variations of the *What Do You Think Of?* game are the use of objects in the classroom, buildings in the neighborhood with which the children are familiar, occupations of people, and so on.

5. Math-Vocabulary Builders

Provide a deck of cards (any kind will do), an egg carton, several shapes of blocks, a pair of something, a breakfast roll.

Questions for discussion:

What are card games played with? [cards, a deck] How *many* cards are in a *deck?* [count them]

What is the *deck* of a ship?

When Mother *buys* eggs at the store they are usually in a *carton.* [examine the carton] How many eggs does an egg *carton hold?* How many eggs make a *dozen?*

Did you ever eat a *stack* of pancakes? How *many* pancakes were there in your *stack?* How many pancakes could be in a *stack?*

What is a haystack? How would you make a *stack* of blocks? How many books must you have to make a *stack* of books?

Do you have *outside* or *inside steps* at your house? How *many* steps do you have? How *high* must you lift each foot to climb your *steps*? Are all *steps* the same *height?*

When you "take a step" *forward, backward, to the right* or *to the left,* how *far* do you go?

Did you ever *roll* down a hill? Can you measure how *far* you rolled? How did you do it?

If your dog knows how to *roll over,* how does he do it?

Do you sometimes have a *roll* for breakfast? What does a breakfast roll look like? [examine] Why do you think it was called a *roll?* Could you make a *roll* out of clay?

There are blocks in this room. Does a *block* need to be any special *size* or *shape*? [examine several blocks of various shapes]

Some people talk about walking a *block* to the store, or five *blocks* to church. What kinds of *blocks* are these? Are they *long* or *short?* [help children to realize the length of a block by mentioning familiar landmarks or buildings that are a block-length apart]

How many things does it take to make one *pair?* What are *twins?* What are *triplets?*

How many people do you see if you see a *couple* of people?

If there are *several* people in the room with you, how many people are there?

How many people does it take to make a *crowd?* Do you know what an *audience* is? How many people are there in the *audience* at a movie? If you go to a circus, you are part of the circus *audience.* How *many* people come to the circus?

6. An Action-word Game

Introduce action words, such as cut, squeeze, roll, chop, draw, color, paint, sweep, dust, burn, slice, peel, ring, dig, unlock, turn, write, print, and so on. Discuss what object or *utensil* is used to *perform* the actions the words talk about.

Line the children up in two lines with an equal number of children in each line. The lines face each other.

Explain that the first child in one line gives his action word to the first child in the opposite line. He must tell what the word uses to *act,* such as roll—wheel, cut—scissors, burn—match, and so on. If he gives the wrong word, or cannot think of a word, he must sit down. The children in the first line continue to give words to the children in the second line until each child in the class has had a turn. The children who have had to sit down may now have a turn at giving each other words.

Listening for Action Words

Read a familiar story to the children, and tell them to listen for *action* words in the story. When a child hears an action word, he should raise his hand.

When the story is finished, the teacher should mention many of the action words, such as *tasted, slept in* and *jumped* in *Goldilocks and the Three Bears.* Who *tasted*, and *what* did she taste? Who *slept* and *where* did she sleep, and so on.

Ask the children to mention action words and discuss them. Make up a story using many action words.

7. Five Happy Days in Kindergarten

A vocabulary activity using time, space, and volume words and expressions; names of days of the week, in sequence; names of meals, family activities, and expressions. This vocabulary activity can be used with the teaching of math experiences.

In a lively class discussion introduce these words:

names of school days
breakfast, lunch, dinner, supper, snack, meal
daylight, sunrise, sunset, sundown
dark, dusk, night, noon, morning, afternoon, evening, midnight
early, late
week, yesterday, today, tomorrow, week before last
never, sometimes, once
little, big
many, few
outside, inside
several, twice, again
every day, every other day, night before last
eve
soon, in a little while, afterwhile, once in a while, next, never
after dark, naptime

As children express themselves about their own activities, add their expressions or words to this list. What did they do *yesterday*, what are their plans for *tomorrow* or *next week?* What did they do *last night, this morning, at noon, after lunch?*

What day is *today?* In a *little while* [or *in a short time*] it will be time to pass out milk and cookies in the room. Is there time to play a game *before* having milk and cookies?

Look at the clock. When the *little* hand points to 10 and the *big* hand points to 6 it will be 10:30, and *time* to go *outside* to play. *Playtime outside* will *last* for *fifteen minutes,* then it will be time to come *inside again.* Do we *always* go *outside* when the clock face tells us it is 10:30?

Days at home:

Were you awake *early* this *morning?* When do you go to bed at *night?* Does your mother ever let you stay up *late?* Do you go to bed at the *same time every evening?* Who gets to stay up after his *regular bedtime once in a while?*

What do we mean by *sundown?* Did you ever get up *early enough* to see a *sunrise?* When does *daylight* come? Can we have *daylight* on a cloudy day when the sun doesn't shine?

Many children have a *naptime every day.* Do you *always* take a nap? Do you *never* take a nap? Do you *sometimes* take a nap? Does your mother ever take you shopping with her *before* or *after* your nap?

What is the first meal you eat, *after* you get up in the *morning?* At your house do you eat *dinner* at *noon?* At your house do you eat *dinner* in the *evening,* or do you have *supper* in the *evening?* Do you eat *while there is light outside* in the *evening,* or do you wait until *after dark?*

In the summer fireflies come out at *dusk* or *twilight.* What *time of day* is *dusk* or *twilight?* Do we have *long evenings* when *darkness* comes *late* in the *summer* or in the *winter?* What *time of year* has *short evenings* when *darkness* comes *very early?*

School days:

What is the name of the *first* school *day* in a *week?* What is the *first* thing you do when you come to school? What is the name of the *second* school *day* in the *week?* [Continue with these questions until all school days have been named and special events have been designated for each day.]

Suggest that kindergartners make picture stories of activities at school, including the *everyday* activities, the *once-in-a-while* activities, and the *special-day* activities. (These picture-stories could be used as a film, in a school-made film box; or as the basis for dramatizations that the children could present before mothers or for other classes in the school.)

Picture-stories of schoolday activities may be displayed in these ways: Use large sheets of oaktag, print the day's name at the top and mount the children's pictures on the sheet. Print *time* words here and there among the pictures. Fasten the five schoolday sheets together and put on an easel, so the children may easily turn each one, like the pages of a tablet.

Another way to use the picture-stories is to fasten the oaktag sheets together at the side with yarn, ribbon ties, or notebook rings. Leave the book on a table for everyone to enjoy.

Use the pictures and make a frieze. Children will like having *time* captions beneath each picture.

The children may want to make pictures and put them into a booklet to take home.

8. Fun with Familiar Words

Introduce this game by saying: "I'm thinking of a *box*. Can anybody give me the name of something that has the word "box" in it? [sandbox, Jack-in-the-box, boxing gloves, or wood box may be a few of the words children will think of]

Next: Give the word "wash," and get "washing machine," "car wash," "wash basket," even "Washington."

Introduce other words the first time the game is played and let the children discuss them, such as, man—manhole, manmade, superman, mechanical man.

bear—bearskin, bear cave, *bare*foot
bed—bed sheets, bedtime
board—chalkboard, boardwalk, all aboard
berry—cranberry, gooseberry, raspberry, blackberry, strawberry
car—carwash, carsick, streetcar
cat—catnip, catfish, cat food
toe—toe shoes, toenail
light—flashlight, light bulb, lightning, cigarette lighter
fire—fireflies, firewood, fireplace, fireman
rain—raindrops, raincoat, rainwater, rainhat

When children have become accustomed to thinking of

new words, they will want to suggest their own word to the class. When choosing a word, the only rule they must obey is to find a simple one so they will know whether the words offered by their classmates are correct.

9. Sound-alike Words

Sound-alike words are often baffling to kindergartners. Use pictures, questions, and discussion to help the children understand the difference between words like steal—steel, mail—male, and so on. From the following list of words choose those that can be pictured, such as mail, mane, tail, herd, reel, deer, hare, pear, and so on.

Show the picture and talk about the mane of an animal; then ask the children what Mother means when she says, "The *main* thing I want you to remember is to look both ways when crossing the street."

Most animals have tails, but a *tale* is something entirely different. What is a *tale?*

Discuss the many ways in which some of these words are used. Cultural and economic backgrounds will determine their meanings to children, and their usage will vary in families. New interpretations for common words will help broaden the understandings of all children in the class.

mane—main	hair—hare
tail—tale	pear—pair
here—hear	rain—rein—reign
herd—heard	ate—eight
their—there	seem—seam
to—too—two	cents—sense
sew—so—sow	die—dye
real—reel	steel—steal
dear—deer	mail—male
rode—road	threw—through

10. Forty Questions

This game will help kindergartners to understand new words and phrases and relate them to their own experiences.

What is the difference between a *pen* and a *pencil?*

Which of these boats are moved by wind—tugboat, speed-boat, sailboat?

If you wanted to make a loud noise, would you *whisper, yell, scream,* or *grunt?*

Why is a rabbit sometimes called a cottontail?

Which one of these train cars does not belong to a freight train—hopper, tank car, dining car, cattle car, freight car?

Which of these story characters are not persons—Goldilocks, Alice in Wonderland, Dorothy, Donald Duck, Tom Sawyer, Pooh Bear?

If Mother buys you a *pair* of shoes, how many shoes does she buy? Does she buy your coats, hats, mittens, pants, shirts, socks, dresses, and boots in pairs?

Would you play football on a court, diamond, gridiron, field, or course?

On which of these would a man play golf—court, diamond, field, course?

How many ways can you eat an egg? [fried, boiled, scrambled, deviled, raw, poached]

A *blizzard* is a big snow storm. What is a *buzzard?*

Three colors are used on stoplights. Name them. What does each color tell a driver or a pedestrian [walker] to do?

How many pennies are there in a dime? How many dimes are in one dollar? How many pennies are there in one dollar?

Would you find penguins living at the North Pole or at the South Pole? [South Pole]

Would you play basketball on a court, diamond, gridiron, field, or course?

Is an ostrich a bird?

Are birds the only creatures that lay eggs? Name some other creatures that lay eggs, but are not birds. [turtles, alligators, some snakes, the Australian platypus]

People use trunks to hold their clothes. How do elephants use their trunks?

If you are five years old now, how old will you be next year? How old will you be in three more years?

Canoe, kayak and *outrigger* are names of three kinds of boats. Indians once used canoes. A Hawaiian might use an outrigger. Who might use a kayak?

Which former president's picture is on a penny?

What kind of a creature did the Ugly Duckling become when it was grown up?

Which of these has the most people living in it—a town, a city, or a state? In which of these do *you* live?

A helicopter is sometimes called a_____? (whirlybird)

Which of these storybook characters ate the baby bear's porridge—Little Red Riding Hood, Tinkerbell, Snow White, Goldilocks? What is porridge? Does your mother ever feed you porridge?

Pinocchio is a storybook boy with a long nose. What living animal also has a very long nose?

A bow is used to shoot an arrow. What is used to shoot a cannon ball? [cannon] What is used to shoot a bullet? [gun] What is used to shoot a stone? [slingshot]

Which is bigger, the sun or the moon? Which is closer to us, the sun or the moon? Which affects the tides of the ocean, the sun or the moon?

What is meant by "full moon"? What does a "crescent moon" look like? Which will give the most light to the earth, a full moon or a crescent moon?

Trains that used steam engines always had a "tender" next to the engine. Do you know why the tender was needed? [The tender held fuel and water. A fireman kept the boiler hot to make steam for the steam engine.]

On a passenger train a man takes the passengers' tickets. What is the man called? [conductor]

A Monarch butterfly is an orange and black butterfly. Monarch is also a name of which one of these people—president, captain, engineer, king? [king]

Which of these animals has no voice—deer, giraffe, buffalo? [giraffe]

A happy person usually does what—frowns, scowls, cries, smiles?

Which of these reptiles changes color to disguise itself—alligator, turtle, chameleon, snake? [chameleon]

How many wheels are there on a tricycle? A bicycle? A unicycle? A tandem?

What would you do at a *rink?* [skate] On a *court?* [play tennis, or basketball] On a diamond? [play baseball] On ice? [skate or play hockey]

Which day of the week is not named here—Sunday, Monday, Tuesday, Wednesday, Thursday, Saturday?

Which of these articles of food cannot be peeled—apple, pear, banana, walnut, peach, plum?

11. Food-word Associations

This game is an excellent one to use when teaching about foods.

Preparation: Provide the children with old magazines and seed catalogs. Ask each child to find at least two of his favorite foods, cut them out, and paste them on construction paper. (These pictures may later on be included in the child's personal "I am_____" book, see chapter 1.)

If suitable pictures cannot be found in magazines or catalogs, they may be drawn and colored or painted by the children. The teacher can furnish pictures from her file of old textbooks, old workbooks, advertisements, and so on.

When all the pictures have been gathered together, use them to discuss foods. Which foods grow *beneath* the ground? Which foods grow *above* the ground? Which foods grow on *bushes?* Which foods grow on *trees?* Which foods come from *animals* and *animal products?*

The children can make posters to show how foods grow; which foods are fruits, which foods are vegetables, and which foods are meats and dairy products. Many city children have never seen peas and beans growing on bushlike plants, or carrots, radishes, or potatoes as the roots of plants growing beneath the topsoil. They have never seen berries on bushes or vines and fruits on trees.

Display the finished posters prominently in the room. Beneath each food print its name and discuss these names at length with the class.

Talk about *dairy products,* which are made from milk. If possible visit a dairy store or a grocery store, and learn the names of various kinds of dairy products, as *skim milk, buttermilk, homogenized milk, half-and-half, whipping cream,* and so on. Learn the more common cheese names.

Use pictures to show children which animals are called

fowl. Talk about the sources of pork chops, ribs, steaks, bacon, and ham. Point out that *hamburger* is not made from ham but is made from beef.

The Food-word Game: Use favorite-food cards, and put them in a stack. Each child may take two pictures, *not his own.*

Tell the children they should study the pictures they hold and make up stories about the foods using information they have learned. Give them ample time to do this.

As each child's name is called, he must stand up and show his picture as he tells a story about a food. These stories are often delightfully imaginative. Sometimes they are simply word-association recitals. The way in which a child expresses himself can reveal much about the child, his thoughts, his likes and dislikes for particular foods, even his emotions.

Food-words and possible associations might be:

onion—hot, green, ring, grows in ground, smelly, Daddy loves 'em, Mom hates 'em.

eggs—boiled, fried, Easter, white, Humpty Dumpty, dozen.

ice cream—cone, chocolate, dessert, sweet, cold, delicious.

Encourage children to use such words such as products, produced, poultry, dairy, leafy, root, dessert, broiled, boiled, fried, toasted, and so on.

12. People We Know Who Do Things, and A Game Called If

Kindergartners should contribute the names of people they know who furnish services to them and to their families as tradesmen, professional people, and others. The teacher can then, from what the children say about the services rendered, list the occupations of these "doers" with whom the children are familiar. There may be many widely conflicting ideas offered about what Mr. Brown, the plumber, does, or what services the president of the bank has to offer.

Occupations of people who do things:

plumber	gardener
baker	caretaker
cook	janitor
storekeeper	zoo keeper

butcher	custodian
mechanic	waiter
farmer	bus driver
taxi driver	doctor
engineer	dentist
housewife	secretary
musician	seamstress
pilot	waitress
president	beauty operator
vice-president	barber
preacher	laundress
priest	stewardess
mayor	nurse
teacher	librarian
rabbi	salesman
lawyer	

Ask children to bring in pictures of people engaged in doing things. (Make sure that ethnic groups are represented in this collection of pictures.) Suggest that they make pictures of members of their own families doing their jobs.

Talk about the need for jobs to provide money for the family needs. Discuss how valuable workers are, and how much each person is needed in his or her own kind of work.

After learning new words that describe workers, introduce this follow-up game of *If:* Begin the game by saying, "If I were a *gardener,* I would use a *hoe,* a *rake,* and a *spade* to make gardens beautiful."

Let the children volunteer to ask questions as each one thinks of a person and describes what objects he would use to work at his job. The teacher can suggest names.

A variation to play, after children become familiar with most of the words in the list, is to have a child mention a name of a worker, such as *engineer,* and ask another child, "If you were an engineer, what would you do?"

Another variation is for the first child to say, "If I use a *needle,* what am I?" The child questioned will then reply, "I am a seamstress [or a tailor]."

Ethnic, cultural and economic backgrounds of kindergartners will determine how many new and unusual words they will contribute in this game of *If*.

13. Words and Phrases That Measure Things

This can be used when teaching math concepts.

Discuss these words, which tell the *size* of things, the *amount* of things, their *place* in *time*, and their relationship to each other; and those that tell *distance* and *space*.

Number

pair	crowd
dozen	less
setting	more
many	triple
several	double
family	trio
class	all
congregation	a lot
audience	heaps of

Size and Quantity	*Place in Time*
pinch	now
smidgen	never
handful	once
medium-sized	again
least	always
most	sometimes
small	ancient
large	olden times
greater	long ago
half	first
third	last
fourth	next
bunch	pretty soon

Distance and Space

close	distant
far away	middle
beside	center
under	in the midst

beneath	beginning
over	ending
above	halfway
beyond	all the way

Note: Setting is a word only rural children might know.

When children have a good understanding of these words, ask them to sit in a circle. Give a word to each child, and ask him to decide if the word tells a *number,* if it tells the *size* of something, the *amount* of something, *when it happened* or *when it will happen,* how *far away* or *how close* something is to him. If the children are undecided, ask them to tell what the word means to them.

14. Big Words from Little Words Can Grow

A game of words that *grow* from the words "house" and "home."

Ask the following questions and let kindergartners choose the correct answers from words the teacher gives them.

If Mother let you make candy at home, was the candy: *homemade* or factory-made?

A person who returns to his home is going: skyward or *homeward?*

A bird whose nest is destroyed is: hungry or *homeless?*

An unhappy child at camp wants to go home because he is: carsick or *homesick?*

A mobile home where people often live is called a: camper or a *housetrailer?*

When you are ill, your doctor may make a: roll call or a *house call* to see you.

Some people have their homes on the water, and live in: speedboats or *houseboats?*

An insect that is a big pest in the summertime is called a: *housefly* or a butterfly?

A lady who takes care of a house is called a: beekeeper or a *housekeeper?*

chapter four

18 Simple Techniques That Bring Dramatic Improvement in Visual Perception

1. Alphabet Recognition Game

On wide brown paper draw the outline of a large elephant. The pictures of other large animals or toys could also be used. Let kindergartners color or paint the picture.

Cut alphabet letters from newspapers or magazines. These letters should be large and black. Paste them on the picture with little space between the letters.

Provide a beanbag.

Place the paper picture on the floor and mark a line where players must stand, some distance from the picture.

Each child gets a turn at tossing the beanbag at the animal. The player must then name the alphabet letter on which his beanbag rests. If it touches two letters, the player must name both letters.

2. How Many Letters Do You Know?

Make a list of all names in the class and display it on an easel. In class discussion ask the children to count all the listed names that begin with the letters A, B, C, and so on.

On the board make columns of these names, each name being listed under the alphabet letter with which it starts. Talk about these names, and their beginning letters. Which letters are almost *never* used as the beginning letters of children's names?

Put a random letter on the board and ask the children to stand if their names begin with that letter. (If some children still do not recognize their own names when they see them, pass out the class name cards, which should be a part of every kindergarten room's teaching aids.) Ask each child to say the name of the letter with which his name begins.

Have children look at the listed names on the board. How many names begin with the letter D? How many with the letter H? Which letters have only one name listed beneath them? Two names? Three or more names?

Mark a large sheet of paper into rectangles. In each space print one of the alphabet letters with which children's names begin.

Collect the name cards the children may be holding. Spread the cards on the table. Ask one child at a time to pick up all names beginning with a designated alphabet letter, such as all the names beginning with R. These names should be put in a stack on the paper rectangle marked with an R.

Continue with the game until all the names are stacked on the rectangles.

3. Letter-hunt Game

Preparation: From newspapers or magazines cut large words that begin with all the letters of the alphabet. Since this is only a beginning *letter* game, the word may be a long one. Let children paste these words on bright construction paper or cardboard.

Use children's name cards, which are part of the room's teaching aids.

Pass out these cards to each child.

Distribute the word cards all around the room, making sure they are on a child's eye level.

Tell the children to walk freely around the room and locate those words whose beginning letters are the same as the letters on their own name cards. They *must not* move the word, but must remember where they saw it, "by the window," "on the piano," "standing on the chalk shelf," and so on.

Ask them to return to their seats when each child has had ample time to find at least one word whose beginning letter is the same as the beginning letter in the child's name.

Call each child by name and ask him to go to a word (or words) he has located. He picks up the word to show the class, compares the beginning letter on the card to that on his name card, then re-places the word.

The teacher keeps score: Donna found 2 words, Bruce 3, and so on.

When each child has reported on his "find," the words are all gathered by the children and are sorted into piles of A words, B words, etc.

The teacher can then check the children's scores and report: "Tommy found *all* the T words," "Lisa found 3 L words and overlooked 1 word," and so on.

As the game is played time after time, each child should find *all* the words whose beginning letter is the same as the one in his name. When a child's score is perfect he loves the feeling of success.

4. A Game of "Can You Find?"

Preparation: Talk about one alphabet letter at a time. Show the children assorted cards on which have been pasted names and objects. Sailboat, Sandwich, Sausage, Squirrel, Sofa, Sun, and Snake are familiar objects. Show the word printed twice, with a capital beginning letter and a lower case beginning letter. Discuss these two shapes of the letters.

Ask a child to arrange the S words and objects in a column on a table. Leave enough room to display other alphabet word-letter cards.

Ask the children to bring in pictures from home that have names beginning with the letter S. Make cards showing these new words and objects.

As new alphabet letters are introduced, ask kindergartners to bring in pictures. Helping find words and making the cards will stimulate letter recognition.

A more difficult version of the game "Can You Find?" —After the children have played the game with the letter recognition cards, display the entire group of words on tables.

Ask children to find names of toys beginning with T, for instance: top, train; of furniture names, such as sofa; of animals, such as B in bear, T in turtle, and so on. When a child is asked to find one or more objects that have names beginning with a certain letter, he must show the card to the class. Include foods, fruits, modes of transportation, and so on among the categories asked for. Children acquire new vocabulary words when playing this version of the game.

Leave these object-word cards on a table so the children can use them in their free time. While playing the game together, some kindergartners learn to recognize simple words and to spell them.

5. Fun with Lower-case Letters

Use three or more wide pieces of cardboard or oaktag cut in strips, 9 x 24 inches. On each wide strip make two black horizontal lines, at least 2 inches apart.

Between the lines on these cards use a black felt-tipped pen to print lower-case letters, making sure the letters touch the lines:

a b c d e f

Display the entire alphabet at the child's eye level. Ask the children these questions:

Which letters have *tails* hanging down below the line?

Which letter is curved like a wriggling snake, and makes a sound like a hissing snake?

If it rained on these letters, which ones would hold water?

Which letters have *only* straight lines in them?

Which letters have both straight and curved lines?

Does an S look like a Z? How is it different?

Does a g look like a q? What difference do you see between them?

A capital Q and a Capital O look almost the same. What is the difference?

Does a lower-case or small q look like a lower-case o?

The letters b and d sound somewhat alike. Do the letters b and d look alike? Show the difference.

M and n also sound somewhat alike. They almost look alike. The letter m has something that n does not have. What is it?

As all the letters are discussed, the children must name

them, point to them, and show their likenesses or differences. In this way children learn to recognize and name the letters out of order. They become aware that each letter is made in a special way. Recognition of the letters is much easier for young children when they have fun learning about them.

Activities: Pass out paper and rulers, if possible. Ask the children to make two lines on the paper with crayons. Then, using crayons, they can make any alphabet letters they like between the two lines, with or without hanging "tails." Ask each child to name the letters he has made.

While teaching the recognition of lower-case letters, the teacher can add interesting features to similar letters, such as b and d, s and z, and so on.

6. An Object-name Recognition Game— "Match the Name to the Object"

Print names of familiar objects and display them in the room, beside, beneath, or on top of the object. Talk about these objects and look at their names. Are the names long ones with many letters in them? Are they short names or medium-sized names? Discuss the beginning letters of each word.

Make duplicate name cards and spread them on a table, stand them along a chalkboard shelf, or otherwise display them at a child's eye level.

Allow each child several turns to go to the table, pick up a name card, and match the name and object elsewhere in the room.

7. Learning the Names of Objects in the Room

Display the names of materials that will be used in the kindergarten room. Print these names the way the children will learn to print them later on.

Use a bulletin board on the child's eye level. Hang up a pair of scissors, a sheet of drawing paper, a box of crayons, a jar of paste, and so on, with the names of the objects printed in large letters.

Talk about these objects and their names. Encourage the

children to say the names. Soon many children will begin to recognize the names without the objects.

Play this game: Use duplicate name cards for each of the materials on display. The teacher keeps one copy of each name, then passes out the other cards to the class. As the teacher holds up a card, the children holding matching cards will walk to the display board and match their words to the correct words and objects.

Another game: Display objects, with their printed names, on a table. Distribute duplicate object-name cards around the room at the children's eye level. Ask children to choose an object-name from the table, then find the matching name somewhere in the room.

8. Word-matching Beanbag Game

Use a large piece of brown paper, 36" x 36" or 36" x 48". Divide it into 6-inch squares with a black felt-tipped pen. In each square paste a picture of an object familiar to kindergartners, such as a house, dog, cat, boat, bear, deer, man, woman, boy, duck, and so on. Leave enough space in each square to print the name of the object.

Make 3" x 7" word cards exactly like the printed words in the squares. Spread these cards on a table so they can be easily seen.

Place the game paper on the floor. Mark a line for players to put their toes on. Provide a beanbag.

Each player tosses the beanbag at a pictured object. He then must go to the table, find the word that matches the word in the square. He shows the card to the class, then returns it to the table.

A more difficult variation of the game can be played when children are more mature: Provide a felt-covered cardboard, 5" x 18" in size. Scatter felt alphabet letters on a table, making sure that these felt letters *exactly* match the shape of the letters used in the game squares.

When a child tosses the beanbag on the game paper, he looks carefully at the picture and its name; then he picks up the correct felt alphabet letters and places them on the felt board, in proper sequence, to match the letters on the game. The child may need to check the order in which the letters must be placed.

This matching game is an excellent one for children to play together in their free time. Alert children love to help slow learners. The children learn to recognize names of common objects easily when playing this game.

9. Name Recognition

Keep children's names displayed at all times. These can be printed on paper balloons with strings attached and arranged on a bulletin board or they can be printed on flowers. They can be printed on real balloons when the class is learning about circuses or zoos.

Print each child's name for him, since he will learn to print it himself later on. Many kindergartners have been taught at home to print their names in capital letters. It may take much playing of name-recognition games to accustom the kindergartner to know his name as Robert instead of ROBERT.

Make folders with the child's name printed on the cover. He can keep his drawings in this folder. Display the children's names on their chairs, if they are assigned to special ones, or on tables where they are to sit to draw and color.

10. A Hand and Name Recognition Game

Give each child a piece of 9" x 12" construction paper. Show the children how to draw around their left hands (if they are left-handed, around the right hand.) Cut out the hand shapes and let the children paste them on colored construction paper. Print each child's name beneath his hand shape.

Ask ten children to stand in a row. Each child holds his hand card in front of him. The class discusses the hand sizes. Which child has the biggest hand? The smallest hand? Choose one child to point out the *three* largest hands in the row. Ask another to point out the three smallest hand shapes.

Use these hand-name cards to play a name-recognition

game: The teacher holds all the cards, and the children sit in a group before her. When she holds up a hand-card, the child recognizes his name, his hand-shape (or both), and stands.

11. Name Hunt

Use two sets of name cards for the class. Ask children to sit in a circle. Give each child his name card. Distribute the second set of name cards around the room, within reach of the children. Give a signal to start the name hunt. Each child must find and bring back to the circle his matching card so he can display both cards to the class.

12. Word Puzzles

Find large pictures of familiar objects whose names have only three or four letters, such as box, boy, girl, dog, fox, cow, pig, top, car, boat, and so on. Mount these pictures on cardboard or oaktag and cut out the shapes.

If an object has a three-letter name, mark the letters with a black felt-tipped pen, then cut the cardboard picture into three pieces and the four-letter objects into four pieces.

Place each puzzle in an envelope made from a fold of 9" x 12" manila paper stapled together at the sides. Put these puzzle folders on a table. Encourage the children to use them in their free time. Soon the puzzles can be removed from their envelopes and the pieces can be mixed together on the table. Kindergartners can be overheard saying, "Where's the front of my dog?" or "Here's a D." "Yes, but that's not *my* D." "I'm making Cat. Who sees the a in Cat?"

Children love these puzzles and learn to recognize shapes, names and they sometimes learn to spell short words!

Colors

13. Interesting Colors

Give each child in the class a piece of 12" x 18" construction paper. Show the class how to fold the paper into a 12" x 12" piece by taking one corner and pulling it down along the opposite side of the paper until a triangle is formed with the

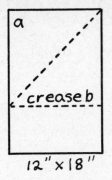

12" × 18"

Take corner *a* and pull it down along the opposite side of the paper until a triangle is formed, where *a* touches *b*. Crease along the diagonal fold.

FIGURE 4-1

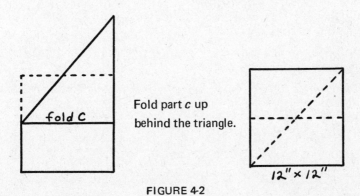

Fold part *c* up behind the triangle.

12" × 12"

FIGURE 4-2

top piece. (Figure 4-1.) Next, show the children how to fold the lower six inches of paper *underneath* the triangle. The last step is to open the fold to make a 12" x 12" space for drawing a picture. (Figure 4-2.)

Lay the papers to one side. Show the class color cards, on which the color name has been printed with a felt-tipped pen of that color. These should be standard room equipment to be used in many games.

Ask the children to express themselves about the colors. Which colors make them feel happy? Which colors make them feel sad? Which colors are summertime colors? Fall colors? Which colors would they see most at the zoo?

After the discussion, ask the children to make pictures with crayons on their sheets of paper using colors they find interesting.

14. My Favorite Colors

Materials needed: Felt-tipped pens for the teacher's use. These pens should be in the same colors as those found in a kindergartner's crayon box.

Give each child in the class a 12" x 18" piece of white construction paper. Show the children how to fold the paper in half. Tell them to use *one side* of the paper to make a picture. They are to use their favorite colors for this picture.

When the pictures are finished, ask each child to *name* his favorite colors. On the blank half of the paper the teacher should print the names of the favorite colors with her felt-tipped pens in those colors. If the child can print his own name, he should. If not, the teacher should print it for him. Display these pictures in the room.

On another day, for a color-learning activity, show the children the color-name cards that are part of a kindergarten room's teaching aids. Ask each child in the class to look at the color names on his own picture. Let him try to match the printed names with the names on the color cards. Remind him that *each name is printed in its own color.*

15. Make Color Puppets

This enjoyable activity will need constant instruction and supervision by the teacher.

Materials needed: Small balloons, both round and elongated in shape; strips of paper towels or newspaper; wallpaper paste mixed with water to the consistency of white sauce; lightweight, flexible cardboard (a suitbox is excellent); an old black boot or shoe, or cardboard to make a boot or a shoe shape.

Procedure: Show children how to "bandage" balloons. Dip strips of paper in the paste solution, gently slide off excess paste with the fingers, and apply the strips to the surface of the balloons. Crisscross the strips several times so there will be at least three layers of paper on each balloon. Allow the paper to dry thoroughly. Let the children make at least eight shapes over round balloons, and two or more shapes over long balloons.

When the balloon shapes are dry, the children can paint them with poster paints to make a *purple* plum, a *red* apple, an *orange* orange, and a *yellow* lemon. Yellow may also be represented with a yellow banana, made from an elongated balloon. Use a large balloon and paint it *brown*. Put eye marks on it and call it a potato.

Add faces to the colored balloons and leaves, hats, clothing or arms and legs, if the children want these puppets to represent people.

A hole should be cut in the base of the figure large enough for a child's hand. The air will escape from the balloons, but the shape will remain rigid, unless accidently crushed. (The extra shapes that were made can be used as replacements.)

Show the children how to make cone-shaped pine trees out of the flexible cardboard. Paint the trees green.

Use an old shoe or boot for the color black. Put a gay, smiling face on it. A child's hand can manipulate this puppet easily.

A large flower can be made from cardboard for the color *blue.*

The puppets are now ready to use.

All the dialogue should be supplied by the kindergartners if the puppets are used in a play. The teacher will need to direct the childrens' suggestions and put them together in some semblance of a story or play.

Children may prefer to present each color, and tell their classmates their thoughts about that color. For example: "*Yellow* is the moon. It's not always round like a circle. Sometimes it's a little moon, like a cut-off fingernail." "*Yellow* is a sour lemon to squeeze for lemonade." "*Yellow* is a banana, but you must peel it to eat it." "*Yellow* is a daffodil. *Yellow* is another flower. It is a dandelion in the grass."

Display the color puppets in the room and use them in many ways.

16. A Color Song to Sing

Sing this song to the tune of "Ten Little Indians."

> Yellow, red, green, and purple,
> Black, blue, brown, and orange,

Colors help *me* make pretty pictures.
I love them, every one!

17. A Bulletin Board of Colors and Foods

Ask the children to bring to school magazines, fruit and vegetable catalogs, and old, discarded picture books. Let them cut out pictures of colored foods.

On a bulletin board display the names of the eight colors most used by kindergartners. Arrange the colored foods around them.

If the children bring in pictures of pink ham, for instance, explain how the color pink is made by mixing two colors together. Discuss the green of peas and compare it to the green of spinach, cabbage, lettuce, green peppers, celery, and so on. Use poster paints and show kindergartners how to make various colors that are all called green but are not alike.

Use the bulletin board display for a game. Place color-name cards around the room. Give each child in the room a *food name.* When the teacher claps her hands the "foods" must go to their own color name card and hold it up.

Use the bulletin board display for an art lesson. Let the children use poster paints or crayons and make pictures using foods in imaginative ways.

18. Games to Teach Color Combinations

Preparation for all color combination games: Display a card on which the names of the three primary colors are printed. Put a large splash of color beside each name.

Provide cans (or ½-pint milk cartons) of poster paints in the primary colors. Provide easels and newsprint.

Let the children discover for themselves how orange is made. One child brushes red paint on the newsprint. Another brushes over the red paint with yellow. What has happened? Ask other children to use red and blue, and blue and yellow, so they may discover how purple and green are made.

Give out art paper and let each child make the color combinations on his own paper. Supply white paint so the children may mix it with the paints to make pinks, lavender, pale green, and so on.

For games 1 and 2 the teacher should provide many color cards with each color name always printed with a felt-tipped pen in its own color.

First Game—Choose one child to be a "caller." Ask the other members of the class to stand in a straight line across the room. Give each child a color card.

When the caller says "Orange" those children holding orange cards will drop out of line and form a small group. The caller says "Orange" again and this time all the children holding *yellow* cards must find a partner who is holding a *red* card. These yellow-red combinations (or partners) stand with the *orange* group.

Next the caller says "Purple" and the children holding purple cards drop out of line. The *reds* that are left in the circle find partners among the *blues.*

When the color "Green" is called, the remaining *blues* in the circle find partners among the remaining *yellows.* Hopefully there will be no colors left over! If there are, ask those children to choose their proper group.

Now line the children up again, still holding their color cards. Ask them how they could make the color *brown.* Show them, with poster paint, that brown can be made by using a combination of *all three* primary colors—red, yellow, and blue.

Explain that black and white cannot be made by using the three primary colors.

Second Game—Color cards are given out as they were in the first game. This time the holder of purple, green, and orange hide in the room, while the holders of red, yellow, and blue keep their eyes closed.

The teacher sings a color rhyme to the tune of "Mulberry Bush."

> Purple is made with red and blue,
> Purple is made with red and blue,
> Purple is made with red and blue,
> Where is purple hiding?

As the last line is sung, the reds and blues in the room must find the purple. Only one red and one blue may remain with one purple. The others must find another purple to join.

The teacher sings the next color combination, and the children proceed as before.

> Orange is made with yellow and red,
> Orange is made with yellow and red,
> Orange is made with yellow and red,
> Where is orange hiding?

Then she sings the last combination:

> Green is made with blue and yellow,
> Green is made with blue and yellow,
> Green is made with blue and yellow,
> Where is green hiding?

If there are any players left, the teacher picks up a *brown* card and sings:

> Brown is made with red, yellow, and blue,
> Brown is made with red, yellow, and blue,
> Brown is made with red, yellow, and blue,
> Join me, all of you!

After playing the game the first time, the kindergartners can sing the words themselves. They learn color combinations easily in this way.

chapter five

29 Fun Games That Teach Number Skills

Counting

1. Attendance Taking (a permanent record)

At the beginning of school make an attendance chart from oaktag. Use it for a month, then make another like it. On this chart print GIRLS and BOYS, with the total enrollment number recorded beside the words. Below them record the attendance for each day in columns.

Appoint a boy and girl attendance-taker or leader for each day. As the teacher calls aloud the children's names from her enrollment book, they stand. Then the girl leader counts all the girls, who sit down as they are counted. (The entire class participates in the counting.) The numbers of girls present and of those absent are recorded each day in two columns beneath the name GIRLS. If there are 20 girls in the class and only 17 girls are present, it is recorded 17 + 3. The class then discusses these numbers and what they mean. On the days when all girls are present a *zero* is recorded in the *second* column. Children are urged to keep the *numerals* in the *first* column *big* by always coming to school. They are urged to keep the numerals in the *second* column *small* by never being *absent*. A *zero* is the ideal figure for the second column.

Attendance for the boys is taken in the same way. The daily attendance record is used for many other activities in the room.

The teacher can stress words and expressions as the attendance is discussed. Are there *as many* girls *present today* as there were *yesterday?* Is there *one less* girl *absent* today than yesterday? Is there *one more* boy *present today* than there was *yesterday?*

At the end of the *week,* check to see if either the girls or the boys had perfect attendance records. Ask who has *fewer* children *absent* this week, the girls or the boys? At the end of *two weeks* discuss and compare the attendance records, do this again in three weeks and at the *end of a month.*

In this way children constantly participate in *counting,* in thinking of numbers as *more than* and *less than* other numbers. They become familiar with the terms *absent, present, one less, three more,* and so on. At this point they may not understand that the record 17 + 3 means that 17 girls present must be added to 3 girls absent to arrive at the *total* enrollment of girls, which is 20; but as they continue to take part in the discussions about attendance, they become aware that numbers may be added together to make another number. They learn that three children were absent on the *first* day of the *week,* but there was only one child absent on the *second* day, so there were *fewer* absent on the second day, and so on.

These daily discussions during attendance-taking are excellent ways to involve children in number awareness. They hear arithmetic terms used, and learn to use them. They become competitive with their own attendance records, trying to keep them perfect. Girls and boys compete with each other to have good attendance records.

Other counting activities: Ask the boy and girl leaders for each day to get enough milk for the total number of boys and girls. Furnish a cart on wheels, if possible, so the leaders must count the entire number of cartons (or bottles) before passing them out to their classmates. How many boxes should the girl leader get for the girls? She can find the correct number on the attendance chart. Soon leaders can recognize any numeral they see on the chart. Counting the boxes as they put them on the cart is a good learning experience.

When children are sitting at tables and need supplies, ask one child at each table to get *enough* paper, for instance, so that *each* child at his table may have *one* piece of paper. He must first count the children and make sure he has *included* or counted himself. This one-to-one relationship between people and objects helps him gain knowledge he will need in other arithmetic experiences.

2. Rote Counting

Use a basketball, or round playground ball. The children are seated on the floor; the teacher stands before them. She bounces the ball several times and asks the children to count the bounces aloud in unison. Let them do this several times. Now ask the children to count the bounces *silently*. Stop frequently to ask for the number of bounces. Are all the answers the same?

Tell the children that the ball will be bounced several times as they count silently, then it will be bounced *to* a child. That child will give the number of bounces he counted. If his answer is correct, he may bounce the ball to another child. Continue until every child in the class has had a turn.

Use the calendar and count the days in a week, the weeks in a month, the days in a month.

Count chairs in the classroom, white keys and black keys on the piano, all the legs on all the chairs at *one* table. Count the chair legs and the table legs.

Count pieces of puzzles.

Count the stars in the flag. Count the flag's red stripes, and its white stripes. Count *all* the stripes in the flag.

Help the children to become aware of objects around them and the joy of counting them, so they will know how many windows there are in the room; how many stairsteps in their own homes; how many buttons they must button on a coat, and so on.

Attendance-taking is also good practice in rote counting.

3. Whose Address Is This? (a home-address recognition game that can also be used as a visual-perception game

Use a copying machine to make requests for home addresses. Ask for street and number, rural route number, apartment number, if any, and so on. Send the requests home with the children.

When these papers are returned, use 3" x 9" oaktag cards (or larger, if needed). Print on these cards the addresses of the children in the room. Use brightly colored felt-tipped markers in all colors except yellow. Ask the child his favorite color, then use it for his address. It will help him to recognize it later on. Print the child's name in the lower right-hand corner of the card.

Pass out the cards to the children and ask them to look at them for a few minutes. Stress that this is something that belongs *only* to him, this is his *own* address, and nobody else in the room has one like it. Ask each child to find something special on his address card that will help him to recognize it. Are there two numerals of the same kind in his house number? Is the name of his street a *long* name or a *short* name? Does the name of his street start with the same letter as his name?

Collect the address cards. Show each address to the class, one at a time. Discuss some special thing about each one, how many words there are in it, how many or how few numerals in the house number, and so on. If possible, make associations between the street name and something else that will make it easier for the child (and his classmates) to remember the address. Does the street have the same name as a former president of the United States? Is the street name an Indian name? Is it the name of some person? Is it named for a flower? Is the name the same as that of some city in the United States? Is its name a number, such as Eleventh Street or First Street? Talk about how streets, avenues, roads, lanes, passes, and so on got their names long ago. Who named them? Why?

Point out to each child that his own name is on his own address card, and they are printed in his *favorite* color. Stress that Bobby and Susan have addresses printed with purple ink, and Karen, Cynthia, and Kirk have theirs printed in red. Continue with the cards until each card has been discussed.

Whose Address Is This? Use the address cards for this game. The teacher holds up a card. "Here is an address printed with blue ink. Whose address is it?"

The child will hopefully recognize his own name in the

corner of the card. If he does not, the teacher may continue to give hints. "This address has 3 numerals, and the first one [or last, or middle] is 9. The name of the street is the same name of a tall, slim tree. Duncan, what does your address say?" Thus prompted, a child will often be able to repeat his entire address.

After a few games of *Whose Address Is It?* each kindergartner should be able to recognize his own home address card and call it aloud.

This game may be used effectively as a dismissal game or to vary the attendance-taking procedure, as well as a math game.

Telephone numbers may be taught to the children in the same way.

4. Have a Real or Pretend Party

Use wooden or plastic spoons, forks, knives; use paper plates, glasses, and napkins. Designate children to be leaders of groups. Each leader should choose five classmates. The group of six children should then set tables for an imaginary party. Talk about the number of spoons, knives and other utensils needed. Collect the materials used after each game.

The next time the game is played, the number of children at each table should differ, with four at one table, seven at another, and so on. This will challenge the children to fit a larger number of chairs around a table.

Vary the game by providing cardboard disks, seeds, and so on to represent cookies on a plate. A child may ask the leader (or hostess or host) to give him one to five cookies on his plate. Provide water so the paper cups or glasses may be half-filled with water.

Another game variation uses a flannel board: The teacher should provide ten spoon shapes and ten plate shapes cut from flannel or felt; provide felt numerals, 1-10. The *host* or *hostess* from each table can go to the flannel board and arrange the correct number of spoons and plates for the guests at his table. He should use a felt numeral to represent the number of *guests*.

Play this pretend game often. Allow immature or timid

FIGURE 5-1
FREEFORM
FOR NAME-THE-NUMBER GAME

children to be leaders frequently. Slow learners may need another child's assistance, but they, too, will benefit from this one-to-one matching and numeral-recognition experience.

5. Name-the-Number Game

Preparation: Use a large piece of oaktag, 24" x 36". On it make freeform shapes to hold 1-10 small shapes. Inside these shapes, in random order, make dots, triangles, or squares using a felt-tipped pen; or bright stickers can be pasted within the freeform shapes. (See Figure 5-1).

Display this game where the children can reach it. Spread the cardboard numerals on a table. Use a pointer. Call a child's name and point to a set of objects. The child names the number of objects in the set, then picks up the numeral representing that number and shows it to the class.

This game should be available to kindergartners at all times. They will enjoy playing it with each other at playtime, with one child taking the role of teacher.

6. Look Around You

Use these questions to introduce the game of *Look Around You:* "How many things in the room are in pairs, or go in twos?" [2 eyes, 2 ears, 2 legs, 2 arms, 2 hands, 2 feet, 2 nostrils, 2 clock hands] "Name all the pairs of objects in the room."

"Can you find things that come in threes?" [3 drawers in

the teacher's desk, 3 buttons on a coat, jeans with 3 pockets, 3 points on a triangle, 3 sides on a triangle]

Continue the game by finding things that are in *combinations* of fours. (Talk about the word "combinations" so the children will understand it.) Find objects that come in combinations of fives up through tens.

4—A square has 4 corners and 4 *equal* sides; desks and tables have 4 corners and 4 sides with 2 *long* and 2 *shorter* sides; desks, tables and chairs each have 4 legs.

5—A person has 5 fingers on each hand; a person has 5 toes on each foot; the flag has 5-pointed stars; the teacher has 5 pennies in her purse, and 5 pennies are the same as a nickel; some kindergartners have been alive for 5 years and are 5 years old.

6—A snowflake has 6 points; insects on display in the classroom have 6 legs each; some kindergartners are 6 years old.

7—The flag has 7 stripes; one child has 7 brothers and sisters; there are 7 dolls in the playhouse.

8—A spider specimen on the insect board has 8 legs; 2 tables have 8 legs all together; 1 chair and 1 table have 8 legs all together.

9—9 boys in the room could make a baseball team; 3 triangles have 9 points all together.

10—Each child in the room has 10 fingers and 10 toes; the teacher has 10 pennies on her desk, and 10 pennies make 1 dime.

7. Members of Families

Use a flannel board for this game, and spread felt figures of men, women, and children on the table so the children may use them (these figures may be cut in sticklike shapes).

Call the children's names, one at a time, and ask each child to select enough felt figures from the table to *represent* the *members* of his family. (Discuss these words to make sure children understand their meanings.) Put the felt figures on the board. When all the figures are arranged, the child will then talk about the members of his family. (Before he has finished arranging the felt figures, a child may ask for cat, dog, bird, or other pet figures to include in his family. He will add these to the other figures.)

When a child has pointed out each member of his family, the children may count the figures. Has the child *included* himself? If not, he should add another child to the family group.

Comment on the family. "Richard [or Ricardo] has 6 persons in his family. He has 2 pets. 6 and 2 make how many members in his family?"

Words that are new to some children are sometimes introduced in these family stories. Discuss aunt, uncle, cousin, stepbrother, stepfather, and so on, if the words are new to the children.

Continue this identification and counting of family members until each child has had a turn to introduce his family and pets. The activity will take several days if the enrollment is large.

This personal participation is an excellent device to use early in the school year when many children find it hard to express themselves before others. When his classmates are interested in what he has to say as he counts and talks about his family members, the child has a warm feeling of belonging to the group. He acquires self-confidence and the ability to talk freely before his classmates.

8. Learning About Sets

Materials needed: Large buttons, plastic spoons, tongue depressors, Popsicle sticks, bottle caps, clothespins, stones, dominoes, small wooden objects from pegboard sets, small blocks, empty thread spools, small plastic animals, felt animals, and a felt board. Small boxes, in which to keep these articles, are necessary. From old magazines or picture books cut out pictures of groups of animals. Make cardboard squares, circles, or freeform shapes, and draw pictures on them or paste pictures on them in sets.

Procedure: Use yarn or cord on a flannel board to make enclosures for sets. Show the children sets of one or two objects. Ask them to use furnished materials and empty boxes, and make sets of one or two objects in each box.

Draw the sets on the chalkboard. Talk about shapes (circles, squares, etc.) on which sets of one or two members have been pasted.

"Does the set of two members *have more than* or *less than* the set of one member?" "Which set is *larger,* which set is *smaller?*"

Talk about sets that are *equal in number.* Use objects, shapes, pictures, and the felt board to demonstrate sets that are *equal in number.*

Explain about one-to-one matching, and remind children that they are doing one-to-one matching when they pass out one milk carton to each child at milk time. Use the words *olden times, long ago,* or *ancient* to tell children about stones or shells having once been used in ancient times as a way of counting before number symbols were used by man.

Explain *equivalent* sets by demonstration on the chalkboard or on paper. Help the children to understand, by their participation in the activity, that *if a line can be drawn from each member of one set to each member of another set with no objects (or members) left over, the sets are equivalent.* Pass out paper to each child and let the children make equivalent sets on the paper, drawing the lines from members of one set to members of the other set.

Introduce sets of three or more members. Ask the children to decide if two sets are equivalent when each set has three members. Show the children, on the chalkboard, how they can *add to* a set of three objects to make it *equivalent* to a set of four or five objects. "How many members were added to the set of three to make it equivalent to the set of four?" Use the terms "more than" and "less than" until they have become part of the kindergartners' vocabularies. *Greater than, larger than,* and *smaller than* are other terms that should be used by children when referring to objects in sets in comparison to other sets.

Help the children to discover, when comparing sets of unequal members, that one set may have *too many members* to match another set. To make *equivalent* or *matching* sets, objects may be *taken away* from the *larger* sets, or *added to* the *smaller* sets.

Introduce dominolike cards (these can be made or bought) to show sets and the numerals that represent them. Let the children use these cards at any time when they have free play.

One-pound coffee cans covered with Contac or construction paper make excellent boxes in which to store all the small objects used in sets. Leave them on a table so the children can use them.

Note: All the materials used in the teaching of sets can also be used when teaching the renaming of numerals.

Recognition of Number Symbols

9. A Flannel Board Game of Number Recognition

Use the flannel board, small figures, and felt numerals. Arrange the figures in sets of 1, 2, 3, etc., and ask the children to put the correct numeral beside the number set it represents.

Remove the sets and scramble felt numerals 1-10 on the felt board. Ask them to arrange the numerals in consecutive order.

Ask one child at a time to go to the felt board and arrange sets of objects beside the numerals.

Arrange sets on the board, 2, 6, 4, 7 in random order. Ask the children to choose felt numerals and put them beside the sets they represent.

Attach a piece of yarn to the felt board to represent a telephone wire. Arrange six felt birds on the wire. Put a numeral 6 beside it. Ask a child to remove two birds from the wire, then ask the question "How many birds are *left* on the wire?" Ask another child to put the correct numeral beside the number of birds *remaining* on the wire.

Continue in this way with all numbers from 1-10. Change the game by *adding to* the number of birds. Encourage kindergartners to use freely the terms *adding to, more than, greater than.*

10. Learning About Telephones

Make a large telephone dial out of two circles of cardboard

or oaktag. On the larger circle print numerals 1, 2, 3, 4, 5, 6, 7, 8, 9, 0. Print the letters, as on a telephone.

On the smaller circle mark and cut out dial circles. Use a long paper fastener to hold the circles together at the center. A small piece of Styrofoam or corrugated cardboard can be inserted at the center between the circles to make dialing easier.

Ask the children if they know how to dial a telephone and let someone demonstrate how to dial from left to right. Ask them to name the numerals on the telephone, and the letters if they can.

Put some telephone numbers on the chalkboard and let children take turns dialing them. Provide toy telephones with authentic dials for playtime.

Ask each child who has a telephone at home to bring his telephone number to school. Play many games with children's personal telephone numbers. Print the numbers on oaktag cards. Each child who has a telephone number should say it over and over until he can remember it. Those children who do not have telephones in their homes may choose the number of a friend to memorize.

A Game of "Who Will Answer?"— One child chooses a telephone card and dials the number, calling aloud the numerals and letters. She asks, "Who will answer?" The child whose number was dialed will rise and say, "Hello. This is Susan." Susan will then choose a card and dial a number. The game continues until each child in the class has a turn. The number cards, when used, are put into a separate stack.

11. Calendar Game

Use a calendar with large, plain numerals, or a teacher-made perpetual calendar.

Each day of the week discuss the name of the day and the number of the day. At the beginning of a new week discuss the week's place in the entire month, such as the *first* week, the *second* week, and so on.

Discuss the number of schooldays remaining in the week. "What is a weekend?" "How many days are in a weekend?" "What are the names of the days when children do not attend school?"

If there are holidays or special days in the week, count the number of days until the holiday. If the special day comes in the last two weeks of the month, count all the schooldays until the special day.

"Who has a birthday in the month?" "What is the date of the birthday?" Mark all birthdays on the calendar at the beginning of a month. Let the children whose birthdays fall in the current month count the days'they must come to school before their birthdays.

Make cards with numerals printed on them *exactly* as they appear on the calendar. Make more than one card for each numeral.

A dismissal game. Stack the numeral cards *upside down,* then give one to each child in the class. Begin with numeral 1 and call the numbers aloud. As a child's number is called, he must show the teacher his card and then point to the correct numeral on the calendar. He may then line up, be dismissed to get his coat and so on. Children who do not recognize the numeral they hold will remain in the room, of course. This happens only a few times, then every kindergartner is alert and presents his card when his number is called.

This game is an excellent one to use as a matching game to test a child's visual perception. Children enjoy it and quite easily learn to recognize numerals from 11 to 31, as well as those 1 to 10 numerals with which they are most familiar. From this game they will also learn that some months have 30, some 31 days, and that February has either 28 or 29 days.

Use the calendar game cards in many other ways. Pass them out, upside down, then divide the class into 2 or 4 groups. Ask those children with cards 1—10 to make one group; those with cards 11—20 another group. Sometimes the numerals 11—19 can be referred to as the "teens," and those numerals 20—29 as the "twenties."

12. Number Rhymes Children Can Make

Read these number rhymes to the children, then ask them to change them a bit and make rhymes of their own that tell about numbers.

Grandpa gave me 1
Water squirt gun.

Grandma gave me 2
Marbles blue.

The dentist gave me 3
Suckers free.

A man sold me 4
Apples at his store.

I saw 5
Bees fly to a hive.

I found 6
Popsicle sticks.

I gave 7
Pennies to Kevin.

I found 8
Stones by the gate.

Here are 9
Cars that are mine.

There are 10
Ballpoint pens.

13. A Game of "A Child Has --- "

Make a child's body outline in the center of a large piece of oaktag. Leave room for pictures and numerals to be added on the sides of the paper.

Supply old magazines and discarded workbooks and ask the children to cut out pictures of legs, feet, arms, hands, eyes, and other parts of a child's body. When pictures have been assembled, ask the children to name the parts of their bodies of which they have only one, such as one mouth, one nose.

Print a numeral 1 (or attach a paper numeral to the chart) and beneath it let children paste pictures of a head, a body, etc.

What parts of the body come in pairs? Print the numeral 2 and beneath it let children paste pictures of ears, eyes, and so on.

Discuss the numerals 3, 4, 5, 6, 7, 8, 9, and 10. Show numeral 5 for five fingers and five toes, the numeral 10 for fingers and toes on both hands and both feet.

Count all the fingers on two children, on four children. Count all the noses in the room. Count all the eyes. Count the hands on the girls. Count all the boys' ears. Children may want their teacher to make a fun chart for these figures.

Keep the figure chart on display. Scatter numeral cards 1, 2, 5 and 10 on a table. Ask one child at a time to pick up a numeral, go to the chart and show that it represents 1 nose, 2 eyes, 5 fingers or 10 toes on two feet.

Add numerals 3, 4, 6, 7, 8 and 9 to the table. Explain that the numeral 3 could represent 2 eyes and 1 nose, that 7 could represent 5 fingers and 2 ears. The numeral 9 could represent 5 toes, 2 eyes and 2 ears. This game amuses kindergartners and they love it. It also introduces them to renaming numerals!

14. A Game of Larger and Smaller Numbers

Introduce this game as a game to be played by two players at playtime.

Many numbered cards are needed—to be divided into two "decks." The numerals may go from 1–30, and the cards can be made of cardboard or oaktag, 3" x 4", with numerals cut from old calendars pasted on them.

Children begin the game by showing the top card from each deck. The child who has the *larger* number on his card takes them both and puts them in a stack. As the game progresses through the deck of cards, the child with the larger number is always the winner. Each child, of course, will win some cards to put in the extra stack. When all the cards in the decks have been shown, the cards in the extra stacks are counted. The child who has the *larger* number in his stack wins. This game should be reversed now and then and the *smaller* number should be the winning number. In this way children will quickly learn the values of numbers.

Encourage quick learners to play the game with slow learners, and enlist their help in insisting that the slow learner *always* decides which is the larger or smaller number.

15. Renaming Numerals

Note: Game number 13, *A Child Has—*, can also be used as an activity when teaching kindergartners how to rename numerals.

Materials needed: Pictures of animals; collections of very small blocks, cars or other toys; beads, spools, plastic spoons, shells, seeds and other objects.

Provide a felt or flannel board and many small felt objects such as pumpkin, star, tree, fruit, bird, and animal shapes.

Remind children that the word "numeral" expresses a number or *stands for* the numbers 1, 2, 3, 4, 5, and so on. The word "number" means *how many* or the total *collection* of animals, objects.and so on. The numeral 2 could stand for 1 star and 1 star. The numeral 2 could be *renamed* 1 and 1 star. (Some kindergartners have observed brothers and sisters doing math and will ask why there is not a plus sign between the 1 and 1.)

Place a numeral 2 on the flannel board, then 2 stars, and the numerals 1 and 1. Ask the children how they have *renamed* the numeral 2. Demonstrate how the numeral 3 may be renamed by using 3 white felt rabbits. Below them place 2 white rabbits. Ask a child to place the proper numeral beside them, which is 2. This is a set of 2. Add 1 more rabbit. Ask a child to put the correct numeral beside the rabbit. "2 rabbits and 1 rabbit make how many rabbits?" "Does the numeral 3 stand for 1 rabbit and 2 rabbits?" "Then 2 and 1 are another name for 3." Rearrange the rabbits, so that each rabbit is alone. Ask a child to put the correct numeral beside each rabbit. "How many rabbits are there all together?" "Does anyone know another way to say 3 besides 1 and 2, and 2 and 1?" "1 and 1 and 1 is another way to rename the numeral 3."

Kindergartners are often able to rename numerals 4, 5 and 6 without too much difficulty. Proceed with renaming these numerals as with 2 and 3, by demonstration, by class participation, by game-playing.

16. Rhymes That Rename Numerals

Rename 2 and 3

2 baby squirrels lived in a tree.
1 was Don and 1 was Dee.
Mother gave them each a nut,
An experience new.
They put them together
And they had 2.

Mother Squirrel watched them.
"I'm hungry," said she.
"I'll find a nut
And that will make 3."
1 nut and 1 nut
Makes 2 nuts, you see.

Another 1 added
Makes enough for all 3.

Rhymes for Renaming 4

2 fish, then 2 more fish
Tommy caught on his hook.
"Here, Mom," he said,
"Are 4 fish to cook."

"*I* want 4 *gold* fish,"
Said his sister Anne.
"To go in our fish tank,
"Not in a pan.
"I've already got 1

"When I go to the store
"I'll buy 3 more
"Then *I'll* have 4."

Renaming 5
5 little ducklings
Swam in the river.
2 ducklings said,
"Turtles make us quiver."
2 ducklings quacked,
"They scare us, too."
1 duckling sat
On a rock in the sun
It took more than turtles
To scare *that* little 1.

5 little puppy dogs
2 black and 3 brown,
Tumbled out of their doghouse,
By a log they lay down.
A boy walked past them
And called to his friend,
"Here are 5 puppy dogs,
Asleep by this log."

Renaming 6: 2 + 2 + 2
A lady raccoon said,
"I have 6 pieces of fish.
"2 I will dip in water,
"2 I will leave for later,
"The last 2 I will eat
Whenever I wish."

2 + 1 + 3
6 little kittens sat in the sun.

What could they do to have
   some fun?
2 grey kittens
Climbed up a tree.
1 yellow kitten said
"I'll go chase a mouse."
3 black kittens played
With a ball of wool.
They would push
And they would pull.
6 little kittens were now having
   fun.
No little kittens were left out in
   the sun.

3 + 3
3 small brown bunnies
Were eating sweet clover.
3 more came along
And said, "Please move over."
3 bunnies and 3 bunnies
Grew round and fat.
If a magician had them,
He'd pull *6* out of his hat!

4 + 2
4 striped caterpillars
Had just shed their skins.
2 more called to them,
"Do you feel the cold wind?"
Each spun a cocoon,
Then 6 cocoons so warm,
Protected the caterpillars,
And kept them from harm.

Geometric Shapes

17. How to Make Teaching Aids

Geometric shapes can be made from the following: (a) *Clay*—rolled out, cut into shapes and dried in the air or baked in a slow oven. (b) *Corrugated boxes* cut into shapes with a razor blade or sharp knife. Glue two shapes together if bulk is desired. Masking tape on the sides can be used to make the edges smooth. These cardboard shapes can be painted or left their natural color. They can be covered with bright Contac paper to make them attractive. (c) *Wooden pieces* in geometric shapes. Obtain these from a lumberyard, or a parent who is willing to cut them from wallboard. Sandpaper these wooden shapes along the sides to avoid roughness or splinters. (d) *Styrofoam*—use Styrofoam balls and sheets. Cut out the shapes with an electric slicing knife or a very sharp kitchen knife. Smooth the edges with coarse sandpaper.

18. Introduce Shapes

Talk about the shapes of geometric figures. Provide triangles with unequal sides, and remind the children that *all* triangles have three sides and three points, but the sides are not always the same length. Use a ruler and let children measure a few triangles' sides to prove this.

A square has four corners, and four sides that *must* be equal. Use the ruler again and mark on it the length of one side of a square. Let kindergartners measure the other three sides. Let them measure squares of other sizes. The ruler, at this point, is used only as a stick on which to mark a length. Inches on the ruler and how to measure in inches should be introduced later.

Examine rectangles with two sides shorter than the other two sides. Children can also measure these rectangles' sides with the ruler.

Talk about circles of many sizes.

19. Geometric-shape Hunt

Children must look around the room to find objects that are circular in shape: clock, ball, balloon, glasses frames, wheels on toys, toy dishes, tops, etc. They may then walk around the room to discover more things having circular shapes.

The next hunt will be for square objects in the room, then objects shaped like rectangles with two sides the same length. If children are undecided about whether an object is a square or a rectangle, help them to measure large objects with a yardstick (not in feet or inches at this point) to get its overall length.

Objects in the room with triangular shapes may be harder to find: a school pennant, blocks, a musical triangle.

20. Make a Chart

Use 24" x 36" oaktag. On it paint or paste colored geometric shapes. Ask children to look in old magazines and catalogs and bring in pictures of familiar objects that have geometric shapes. Let them paste these pictures on the chart and label them. Keep the chart on display in the room. It can be used for a game.

Toss and Match—a game played on the floor with the chart. Mark a line on the floor where the children must stand. Give them a beanbag for the game. A child puts his toes on the line, names an article pictured on the chart (which is on the floor), then tries to hit the object with the beanbag. If he misses the object he mentioned and touches another he must tell the shape of the one he hit with the beanbag. If a child really hits the article he named, he gets one point.

21. Talk About Geometrically Shaped Foods

Children are surprised to realize that many foods have geometric shapes. Ask them to think of foods shaped in:

> *Circles:* cookies, pancakes, some crackers, oranges, plums, peaches, macaroni, lunch meats, biscuits.
> *Squares:* crackers, Jell-O servings, sandwiches, pieces of cake.
> *Triangles:* pieces of pie, sandwiches, slices of cake and so on.
> *Rectangles:* crackers, cake, ice cream bars, cookies, slices of bread, loaf of bread, etc.

Make a chart of foods that have geometric shapes. Name the shape as "circle," with a circle beside it, "square," and so on. Ask children to bring in or draw food pictures to illustrate the chart.

22. Matching Game

Use the charts already made of foods with geometric shapes or just plain geometric shapes. Let children make cards with geometric shapes on them. Pass out these cards, one or more to a child. When his name is called he must *match* his card to the correct shape on the chart and *name* the shape.

Teaching Ordinals

Terms

Kindergartners need to understand *ordinal* numbers, which indicate order in a specific series. All kindergartners know what it means to be *first* in line, *first* to be served, *first* on the slide, and so on. The words *next, in between, middle, last, next-to-the-last* refer to the order of things, but do not represent numbers. Discuss such terms with the children before introducing ordinals.

Line up children in the room using the words, "You're *next* and you may stand *behind* Tommy. Mary, I'll put you *between* Robert and Suzanne. Charles, you may be the *last in line* because you are the tallest boy. Billy will be next-to-the-last in this line." On the playground arrange races and games where children run first, last, take turns later, or next, or after a while.

Introduce ordinals by lining up ten children across the room. Point to and name each child, "Carol is *first*, Maria is *second*," until all ten children have been named.

Activity 23. Learning to Line Up

(1) Carol stands at one end, the *first* child in the line; Ricardo is the *last*, or *tenth* child in the line. The line is *facing* the rest of the class. Point out to the children that position in line always begins at the left and goes from *left to right* just as stories are read from left to right. Call a child to stand in front of the *second* child in line, the *fourth* child, the *ninth* child, etc.

(2) Now line ten more children in a straight line, one child *behind* another. Designate first, second and so on, showing children that in a line like this one, the first child is at the head

of the line, or where a game *begins.* The *last,* or *tenth* child is at the *end* of the line where the game *ends.* Play a similar game of "Go stand *beside* the *seventh* child," and so on.

Activity 24. Position of Stairsteps

Draw stair steps on the chalkboard. Explain that steps going up begin with the *first* step at the *bottom.* "Where would the *last* step be?" "If a person were upstairs and wanted to come down, where would the *first* step be?" "At the top of the stairs, of course. Then the bottom step would be the *last* step."

Activity 25. Climb an Imaginary Stairs

Let children use felt figures to represent themselves and climb the stairs on the chalkboard. (There should be at least ten steps.) As a child lets the little figure climb, the teacher stops him and he must tell her if he is standing on the second, third, or sixth step. Other children may use the little figures to come *down* the stairs, always naming the step on which they were stopped.

Activity 26. Learn About the Flag

"Look at the American flag. Count the stripes beginning at the top." "What is the color of the *first* stripe?" "The *second* stripe," etc.? *Every other* stripe is white, they will discover. Make sure the children understand the term *every other,* which is used in many homes. "Name the rows of stripes beginning at the *bottom* this time."

Point out that some of the stripes in the American flag are beside the field of stars. "What is the position name of the stripe *under* the field of stars that goes from one side of the flag to the other?"

Activity 27. A Game to Learn Sequence of Ordinal Numbers

Make sure that kindergartners understand the sequence of ordinals, just as they understand the sequence of numbers. With chalk draw ten circles on the floor. Number them 1–10. Call the names of children to stand in circle 1, circle 2 and so on. Do they understand that circle 1 is, in this case, the *first* circle? Call children to stand in the first, second, and following circles in sequence. The second time around ask children to stand in the circles in random order, the fifth, the eighth, the second and so on. Repeat this game until all have had a turn.

Activity 28. A Circle Game with Ordinals

Make a large circle on the floor with chalk. Mark it into halves and each half into fifths, so there are ten spaces. Number these spaces from 1–10. Choose ten children to play and tell them to stand in the ten spaces on the floor. The teacher plays the piano, or plays a record. When the music starts, the children begin to skip around the circle. When the music stops, each child must look at the spot on which he stands. The numeral on it should tell him his ordinal position, whether tenth, sixth etc. He tells his teacher his position. Let each child in the class have a turn to play.

Activity 29. Musical Chairs

Line up ten chairs in the room, one behind the other. Make sure the children understand which chair is the number 1 chair, or the *first* chair. Scatter numerals about on a table.

Choose ten players. Tell them that they must march to music around the chairs. When the music stops, each child sits in a chair. He must then count (silently), beginning at the *first* chair, to find his position. When the teacher claps her hands, each child goes to the table and finds the *numeral* that represents his *ordinal* position in the row of chairs. He must name the numeral and also his position in the line of chairs.

This is rather difficult game and at first only the more mature kindergartners may want to play. Soon others will ask to be included. Children love its challenge to their knowledge of numbers and their order; they are proud of their knowledge of the relationship of numbers and ordinals.

chapter six

27 Successful Ways to Teach: Time, Measurement, Money Values, and Spatial and Relational Concepts

What Is Time?

1. Terms

Young children think of time as "Time is dinner time," "Time is when I go to school," "Time is after a while," and "Time is when Mother says, 'Not now, I don't have time.'"

Listed below are common words and expressions that are used by children and their parents to express time without using a clock. Print them on oaktag and talk about them with the class. Ask the children which expressions of time are commonly used in their homes, as "in a jiffy," "as soon as," "a long time ago," "in olden times," and so on. They will contribute interesting ethnic or colloquial expressions, which can be added to the list.

before	after lunch	daily
noon	never	evening
night	late or later	sometimes
again	today	in a little while
once	dusk	in a minute
twice	twilight	after a while
morning	after dark	always
early	long ago	once in a while
yesterday	sooner or soon	nap time
tomorrow	every day	

Read stories about time, for example, *A House for Willie*, a

Golden Press Book, by Jane Britten, New York: Western Publishing Co., Inc., 1971.

Print some simple time words on 3" x 9" cards and let the children look for them in stories about time.

2. Clocks

Have the children make large clock faces for the front covers of booklets. Pages for the booklets can be cut in the same circular shapes as the covers. On these pages, the children can draw pictures of special times in their own days that are important to them. They may want to print, or have the teacher print, some time words on these pages. Fasten the booklet together with string, yarn or paper fasteners.

Seasons Tell Time

Note: Time can be defined, in this frame of reference, as "period," "season," "summertime"; as a more or less definite portion of duration characterized by particular events or circumstances; as a case of recurrence or repetition, and so on. Children think of the seasons as telling the time to go to school, time for school to be out, time for new animal babies, and time for snow.

3. Fall

Seasons are nature's way of telling time. Introduce the idea of seasons to the children and ask these questions:

When does school begin? (September is the *first month* of *fall.* Stress these time terms in the discussion.)

Did Mother provide any special clothes for you in the fall?

Do animals change in any way in the fall? (Animal fur becomes very thick. Squirrels gather and hide nuts. Chipmunks and ground squirrels store up food.)

Do insects make preparations for fall? (Before insects die in the fall, they lay eggs. These will hatch into baby insects in the spring. Butterflies and some other insects lay eggs that hatch into caterpillars; these make chrysalises in which they spend the winter. In spring, they change to butterflies. See chapter 7 on nature.)

What do butterflies do in the fall? (See chapter 7. A few butterflies hibernate in the fall. Monarch butterflies fly south in the fall. Most butterflies lay eggs that hatch into caterpillars.)

How do trees change in the fall? (Leaves turn beautiful colors and fall to the ground.)

What special things must people do in the fall? (Rake leaves, cut wood for winter in some parts of the United States; store vegetables, and fruits and grains in some states.)

What is one exciting special time in the fall? (Halloween)

Columbus Day comes in the fall. Who was Columbus?

What is the name of the feast day we celebrate in the fall? (Thanksgiving)

4. Winter

Discuss winter, its weather, and how the earth's season has changed from fall to winter. Name the holidays in winter. "What new kinds of work must people do around the house in winter when it sleets and storms and there is heavy snow?" Make a list of questions about winter to discuss in class. Make pictures or a frieze for the room to show this season and the ways in which children enjoy winter.

5. Spring

What are some of nature's changes in the spring? Discuss holidays in spring and its new life among animals and insects. "Must children wear different clothes in the spring than those they wore in the winter? Do some people's jobs change in the spring?" (Farmers, vegetable growers and construction workers are among those whose jobs change from winter to spring. Let children freely discuss changes in their homes and lives in the spring.)

6. Summer

Summer for some children is a time spent on the beach, for others it is spent in frequent trips, or visits to relatives. Children go to camp and to public parks. They have unlimited time to play. Make charts showing the way each season tells a time to do certain special things in your school, in your home, and in your community. Children will enjoy making drawings of the four seasons' activities.

Calendars Tell Time

7. Months

Use a large calendar with large, plain numerals. Explain why there may be 30 days in some months, 31 in others and either 28 or 29 in February. Tell the children about the number of days in an entire year and introduce the twelve months in the year by name. (See chapter 1 on teaching aids for ways to make calendars.)

Discuss the name of the month in which children are learning about time. "How many days are there in *this* month?" "Who has a birthday in *this* month?" "What is the *number* name of your birthdate?" "How many days will there be *until* your birthday *this* month?"

Introduce the months in sequence, and talk about each, including the number of days in each month. Identify each month with the season to which it belongs. Review the important events or holidays that occur in each month. Talk about the *first* month, the *second,* and so on. Explain that months can tell the time of year, just as seasons can tell the time.

8. Weeks

Use the current calendar month when introducing the number of weeks in a month. Then look at other months on the calendar. "Does a month *always* have *four* weeks?" Find months that have five weeks, or a *few days* in a fifth week.

Count the days in a week. "What is the name of *today*?" "What is the name of *yesterday*?" "Of *tomorrow*?" Discuss the names of all the days of the week and identify Sunday as the *first* day, Monday as the *second* day and so on. "Are the names of the days of the week *always* the same in every month?"

Go over calendar facts with the children until they are quite familiar with the names of the days of the week and the names of the months of the year. Encourage them to say, "Tomorrow is Tuesday," or "Friday is the last day we will come to school," or "Saturday is the last day of this week."

9. A Game of Which Comes First?

This game can be played with the names of the seasons, the names of the months or the names of the weeks. Assign names to children and, if the whole class is to play at once, assign several Mondays, Tuesdays, etc. Now call out, "Which day comes *first* in the week?" and all the Sundays will come to the front of the room. "Which comes *second*?" will bring all the Mondays to stand beside the Sundays.

Use the Matching Game also. Make 4" x 4" oaktag cards and on them print numerals exactly like those on the calendar being displayed in the room. Make one each of numerals 1-10; make two each of numerals 11-31.

Turn numerals upside down and pass them out to the class. Some numerals may not be passed out at all; there may be two of the same passed out.

The first time this game is played call out the numerals of the calendar in consecutive order. As a child matches his numeral by name and by sight, he brings it to his teacher.

After this matching game has been played a few times, the teacher does *not* name the numeral but points to it with a pointer. The child must name it as he matches it to the numeral he holds in his hand. Soon kindergartners will be able to match the numerals they hold to those on the calendar when the teacher points to them in random order. They will also learn to name all the calendar numerals in random order.

This game is an excellent one to teach number recognition, the number of days in a month, to test a child's attention, to test his auditory and visual perception, and to teach him new conceptions of time. It is also a *great* favorite with kindergartners!

Some terms to talk about are:
tonight or tomorrow
tomorrow or the next day
day after today

day after tomorrow
day before yesterday
five days from now
in two weeks
half a month

Clocks Tell Time

10. Learning About a Clock Face

Provide old clocks or watches for kindergartners to examine. If the glass covering is removed children can then examine the raised numerals and turn the hands.

Make a number of clock faces from firm paper plates. Plastic soda straws fastened to the center of the face with paper fasteners make good clock hands. The numerals should be printed with black and should match the numerals on the classroom clock if possible.

Ask children to name all the kinds of clocks they have seen; name all the places where they have seen clocks. Why were there clocks in these places? Why do people own clocks and use them?

Set up an imaginary situation concerning the kindergartners and their school—what if nobody used clocks to tell the time of day? Without clocks how would all the children know when to come to school so they could be together? Would the teacher get there at the same time as the children? Ask them to help make a list of all the people who used clocks or watches so children can come to school at the same time.

How is the classroom clock used? Make a chart of events that happen every day in the classroom. Discuss them.

11. Using Clocks

Pass out paper plate clock faces so two children can use them together. Tell them to look at the classroom clock then set their own clock hands to match. Use these clock faces often during the day when activities change in the room.

When milk is served, what do the clock hands say?
When the clock hands point to_____and_____we
  will have playtime.

Set the play clocks at that time.

The clock hands now point to_____ and_____.”

"They say_____.”

Set your clock hands.

In fifteen more minutes the clock hands will point to _____ and_____. The time will then be _____.

When the clock hands point to_____ and_____ it will be rest time.

Rest time will be over when the clock hands point to _____and_____and the time is_____.

At_____we will be ready to go home.

Make sure the children always turn the clock hands in the correct direction when using the clock faces. With this kind of meaningful play children are constantly aware of the clock, the way in which its hands move and of the need to use a clock for accurate time-telling.

Give each child a paper plate and let him make his own clock face. Point out the position of the 12, the 3, the 6, and the 9 on the clock face and have the children make these numerals first, then add the other numerals in between. The hands may be made of soda straws, cardboard, oaktag or construction paper with a paper fastener to hold them in place.

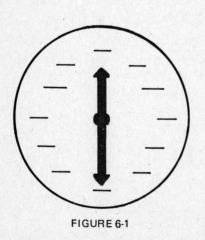

FIGURE 6-1

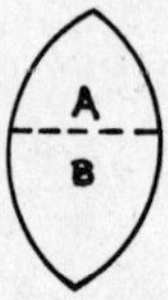

FIGURE 6-2
Bend tab *a* forward on line.

FIGURE 6-3
12—Print numeral here
Paste part *b* of this tab to part *b* of first tab.

12. A Clock Face Game to Play

(Hang this clock face on the wall within reach of the children, or place it on the floor.)

Make a large oaktag or cardboard clock face. Paint it or cover it with Contac paper or cloth. Add hands. Make horizontal slots in the face. (See Figure 6-1)

Make tabs. (See Figure 6-2) Bend the tab part *a* forward so when tab part *b* is in the slot, *a* will hold it there.

Make numeral tabs exactly like the other tabs. (See Figure 6-3) Print numerals 1–12 on these tabs exactly like the numerals on the classroom clock. Paste part *b* of the numeral tab to part *b* of the first tab.

Give out the 12 numerals to children. Call them in clockwise sequence for a few times until each child has had a turn to place his numeral in its proper slot on the clock face.

Next give out numeral tabs 12, 3, 6, and 9. Let the children put them in the proper slots. If the clock face is on the floor, children can then stand beside the numeral.

Give out 1, 4, 7, 10 first, so the children can place them on the clock face, then give out numerals 2, 5, 8 and 11.

After children have played the clock face game many times, try a more difficult version. The clock face is on the floor. Give children only *verbal* numbers and ask them to take their proper "clock" positions without seeing any numerals on the clock face.

Measurement

13. Terms

Relating measurement terms to the experiences of many kindergartners is important to their understanding of these terms. The following list of words and expressions should be discussed before the class measurement activities begin and should be used by teacher and children as learning progresses from one phase of simple measurement to another.

| empty | most | fewer |
| full | a few | many |

enough	triple	handful
less than	single	team
more than	trio	family
narrower than	fewer than	dozen
smaller	size	pair
larger	weight	half-dozen
taller	amount	group
as long as	exactly	duet
as wide as	one for each	twin
compare	enough for all	heavier
height	too much	lighter
length	not enough	both
set	enough	close to
crowd	wider than	grown
flock	width	half-grown
herd	same	full-grown
collection	class	blocks
double	deck	miles

14. Size

Let children discover for themselves the differences in the sizes of objects, as they *compare* chairs, toys, the *height* of windows and doors, the sizes of children, the *length* of their fingers, the *size* clothes Mother buys for them. (This information needs to come from home.) Compare sizes of blocks, the length and thickness of the fish in the aquarium, the *length, width* and *thickness* of books on the table.

A question to discuss: When two objects (blocks for instance) are exactly the same height but are not the same width, do *wider* objects look *taller* or *shorter* than *narrow* objects? (Show the class some blocks that are exactly the same height.) Kindergartners enjoy such "think" questions.

Draw four rectangles of the same size on the chalkboard, or on a large piece of oaktag. On the first rectangle make vertical lines, on the second one make horizontal lines, divide the third one into diagonal shapes and put a freeform design on the fourth one. Fill in every other space on the second rectangle and fill in two of the triangles on the third one.

Ask children to look at each rectangle and then decide which is the *largest*, the *next in size*, and the *smallest*. Ask them to point out any rectangles that are the *same* size. When each child has given his opinion, discuss the reasons why the rectangles *seem* to be different in size when they are really the same size. Use a ruler to prove that this is true. Give children lengths of string or yarn and let them measure books that *appear* to be the same length but may not be.

Introduce and talk about a ruler and a yardstick. Kindergartners need not concern themselves with inches and feet; some mature children will want to use inches and feet in their measurement of objects in the room. They can have special instruction if they have not already learned about inches and feet at home.

Encourage kindergartners to measure things in their free play. Suggest all kinds of things that can be measured.

If children become interested in shoe sizes, draw around the feet (or shoes) of several children. Make a chart to display in the room showing shoe or foot sizes.

Measure the height and weight of each child in the room. On a chart beside the child's name record these facts: height, weight, age, shoe size, mitten size, dress, shirt or slacks size, coat size. Some of this information must come from home. Children are very proud of their individual identification with the size-measurement learning activities.

15. Things Can Be Measured in More Than One Way

Take kindergartners who attend school in the morning outside early on a sunny day and again as close to noon as possible. Talk about the shadows they make early in the morning. Discuss the *length* and *size* of the shadows they make just before noon, when the sun has changed its position. Measure the shadows with a yardstick. Suggest that these children measure their shadows at home in the middle of the afternoon and again just before sundown. (Note: These *time* expressions are helping children to be aware of the time of day and how it directly affects them.) Ask them to have some member of their family write down these measurements so they may bring them to school.

Children who attend kindergarten in the afternoon should measure their shadows right after breakfast, then just before school time in the afternoon.

16. A Measure-and-Jump Game

Use cardboard boxes (shoe boxes are excellent) and put one in the center of the floor. Children can then measure its depth, or distance from the floor with a ruler as "this far" or, more accurately, in inches.

Children line up to take turns jumping over the first box. When every child has had a turn, add another box to the first one and measure the height of both boxes. As the children continue to jump, add another box to the stack and measure. Continue until there are several boxes in the stack. If a child, while jumping over the boxes, knocks the top box down, or knocks most of the boxes over, he must sit down until the game is finished. The game ends when the box pile is too high for any child to jump over it.

This competitive game of *Measure-and-Jump* is an excellent one to use when children are tired and need exercise.

Note: Read some stories to the children that talk about the sizes of things. *Cecily G and the 9 Monkeys,* by Hans A. Rey, Boston: Houghton Mifflin Co., 1942 is an excellent book to read. Another good measurement story is *Inch by Inch,* the story of an inchworm, by Leo Lionni, New York: Astor-Honor, Inc. 1962.

17. Weight

Weigh each child on the school scale and record his weight in pounds and ounces so he can learn the terms. Ask children to lift familiar objects in the room and decide which is the *heavier* toy, ball, book and so on. Give them a teaser question: Is a ball of twine *lighter than* or *heavier than* a ball of yarn the same size? Provide two balls for them to lift *after* they have answered the question.

Give them two more balls of the same size, one of Styrofoam and one of rubber. Which ball is the heavier? Let them compare the weights of these balls with the balls of twine and of yarn.

Send notes home with several children asking for small quantities of flour and sugar. Measure exact amounts of the flour and sugar and place them in paper cups. Ask the children to guess which *weighs the most,* the flour or the sugar. If possible provide a small scale and let the children watch while the cups are weighed. Tell them the exact weight in ounces.

Show them a feather and a pencil of the *same length.* Which looks heavier? Examine coats and boots belonging to children. Why are some boots heavier than others? Why are some coats heavier than others?

Talk about the weights of animals. Many kindergartners have seen polar bears at the zoo. Measure a space in the classroom 9 feet in length. Tell the children that a *grown* polar bear is often 9 feet long, *as long as* the space in the room. He may weigh close to 1,600 pounds, which is almost a ton; but when he was born, he was *no bigger than a small rabbit!*

Kindergartners have seen hummingbirds at some time or other. A *grown* ruby-throated hummingbird weighs *less than a copper penny.*

Talk about how much babies weigh when they are born. How much did the newest baby brother or baby sister weigh? The children may want to bring notes to school telling how much they weighed at birth. If possible, compare these weights with something ordinary and familiar as a ten-pound bag of sugar or flour, or other articles that the teacher can bring to school. Let the children lift them or lift a five-pound bag of flour *and* a pound of oleo or butter at the same time, to get the feel of six pounds of weight.

Ask children to look at one stick of butter or oleo, which weighs four ounces, then lift it in their hands. Tell them about a full-grown flying squirrel, which is about as long as a foot ruler if measured from nose to tip of tail, but weighs only as much as the stick of butter—four ounces.

Suggest that the children ask their mothers to help them find cans of food that have their weight on the labels. Compare the sizes of empty food cans. Are there cans that, when they were full of food, *weighed the same,* but *were not the same size?* Can the children figure out why this is true?

Kindergartners can acquire an understanding of the differences in the weight of various foods and will enjoy reasoning out little problems about comparative weights and sizes. Relate all such experiences to common and familiar objects when possible.

18. Quantity

Terms: Families express quantities of things in a variety of ways. In a class discussion about familiar things that children eat, drink, handle, wear and live with, many colloquial or ethnic words and expressions will be added to the following:

buckets of	teaspoon
loads	number of
a cupful	a pailful of
heaps	a dollop of
handful	several
bunch	couple of
a lot	gallons
a few	half-gallons
drop	quarts
smidgen	half-pints
pinch	cups
amount	half-cups
pints	portion
tablespoon	

19. Questions and Answers to be Discussed

If I gave you a *couple* of oranges, how many oranges would you have?

I ate *several* cherries. How many did I eat?

If Mother runs a *bathtubful* of water for your bath can you tell me how high the water comes up in the tub? [bathtubful is not a word, but is used as such in many households]

If you have *heaps* of pennies in your bank, how many pennies do you have?

Your friend Bobby says he has *a whole bunch* of new toys. How many new toys does Bobby have?

I will give you a *handful* of peanuts. How many peanuts are there in a handful?

Mother put three *drops* of red cake coloring in the cake icing. How did she measure the drops?

Some foods have a *teaspoon* of salt in them. How can you measure a teaspoon of salt?

How could you measure a *pinch* of salt? Would *your* pinch of salt be as big as a grownup's pinch of salt?

Let the children help make drawings to illustrate the words underlined in the questions. *Several* can mean more than two objects; *heaps* of things can actually mean heaps or piles, but it can also mean a large number; the size of a *handful* can depend on the size of a person's hand; a *drop* of red coloring is what really comes out of the special dropper cap on the bottle; *measuring spoons* of various sizes are used to measure a teaspoonful, etc; a *pinch* of salt is the amount of salt that can be held between two fingers and the amount may vary in size as people's fingers vary.

Provide measuring cups and half-pint, pint, quart, half-gallon and gallon containers. (Milk cartons are excellent.) If there is no sink in the schoolroom provide a large pail of water and two large containers for water. Let children fill these milk-carton containers with water, then empty the amounts of water into other containers so they can make comparisons between them.

20. Bring Measuring Cups and Measuring Spoons to School

Use water or dry cereal like oatmeal and let children discover for themselves that 4 of the quarter-cup measures, when filled with something, will fill the cup measure or will equal the cup measure. Let the children experiment freely, perhaps mixing the liquid and dry materials, then measuring again to see if the thick liquid made any difference in how much could be put into a container.

If the children are interested, make charts to show the relationship between the spoon sizes, cup sizes and other containers that measure quantities of materials.

Ask children to bring empty food cans with labels, then let them discover how much water each can will hold in cups, parts of cups, half-pints, pints or quarts. Read the labels on the cans to the children so they will have a better understanding of quantity.

21. Wholes, Halves, Thirds, and Fourths

Teaching aids for this activity can be made (see chapter on teaching aids) or bought (from school supply houses). Use wooden plates of fruit with apples, oranges and pears cut into halves, fourths and thirds; or use paper plates divided in the same way. Large fruit shapes can be made and divided for use on the felt board. Cardboard shapes are also effective in helping children to learn how objects may be divided into halves, thirds and fourths.

Use real fruit for demonstrations when possible and let children eat the portions after the fruit has been divided. Kindergartners easily grasp knowledge of the ways in which objects may be divided.

Tell a story like this: "One day I had a bowl of fruit and in it were oranges, peaches and pears. Molly and Steven came to visit me. (Use names of children in the class.) I told them they could each have a piece of fruit. They both wanted an apple and I had one apple in the bottom of the fruit bowl. How could I give *one* apple to *two* children?"

Some child will probably suggest that the apple can be cut in two. What does it mean to cut an apple *in two?* When the children show the teacher how to do this she can then cut the apple into two pieces. Does anyone know what these pieces are called? Talk about *whole* objects that can be divided into *halves,* or into two pieces and that each piece is *one-half* of the whole object. Continue with the story, using the names of the children and introducing fourths and thirds.

Use a paper plate to show children how to divide a whole object into halves, then into fourths. Demonstrate to them that a paper plate can be divided into thirds by making a big, open Y, then cutting along the lines.

Pass out paper and one can lid to each child in the class.

Ask them to draw around the lid and make three circles on the paper to look like three whole objects; then cut out the circles.

Divide the first circle into *halves.*
Divide the second circle into *fourths.*
Divide the third circle into *thirds.*

Young children who are members of large or medium-sized families can easily comprehend the need for dividing one whole thing into many pieces and they learn quite easily to do this themselves.

Place wooden fruit, paper plates, paper, can lids and scissors on a table so children can use them for free-time play.

Money Values

22. The Use of Real Money Teaches Money Values

Pennies are used in some parking meters, in penny banks and so on and most young children know these things about pennies. Help them to learn additional facts about pennies:

It takes as many pennies to make a nickel as a child has fingers on one hand.
It takes as many pennies to make 2 nickles as a child has fingers on both hands.
It takes as many pennies to make 1 dime as a child has fingers on both hands.
It takes 2 nickles to make 1 dime, but a dime is smaller in size than a nickel.

Play a little game. Pretend that each finger is one penny. Close the fingers of one hand into a fist. The fist is now *5 pennies,* or *1 nickel.* Close the other hand into a fist. The child is now holding five (pretend) pennies in each hand or a (pretend) nickel in each hand. He has how many pennies all together? How many nickels has he altogether?

It takes *ten pennies* to make *1 dime.* How many nickels does it take to make 1 dime? Use the fingers and hands to demonstrate.

Set up a little store in the classroom. Children can supply

empty cans, empty cartons and boxes to use as merchandise. Give them play money or cardboard disks and let them "shop" at the store.

Children can plan and put on a play for which they will charge admission. They can take a pretend ride on a bus and pay their bus fare with pennies, nickles or dimes.

23. Play a Game of Name the Number

Ask children to stand in line across the room. They must *name the number* as they answer these questions:

A nickel is how many *pennies?*
A dime is how many *pennies?*
A nickel is how many *cents?*
A dime is how many *cents?*
A dime is how many *nickels?*

Each child in the class should have one or more turns at naming the number of pennies and nickels.

24. A Game of More or Less or the Same

Ask these questions for this money-values game:

Is a penny more or less or the same as a nickel?
Is a nickel more or less or the same as a dime?
Is a cent more or less or the same as a penny?
Is a cent more or less or the same as a dime?
Is a cent more or less or the same as a nickel?
Are ten pennies more or less or the same as a dime?
Is a nickel more or less or the same as five cents?
Is a nickel more or less or the same as five pennies?
Are two nickels more or less or the same as one dime?
Is a dime more or less or the same as ten pennies?

Spatial and Relational Concepts (to help children understand the connection between people and things and between objects and other objects)

25. Terms

Children should become familiar through discussion with these spatial and relational words and phrases:

close to	under
away from	right
beyond	left
below	fat
above	thin
in between	along
in the middle	follow
center	lead
around	*all* ordinals
inside	long
outside	short
big	small
bigger	large
biggest	*all* names of
together	geometric shapes
apart	heavy
on	light
in	thick
over	thin

Add to this list as children express ideas about the connection between people and things and between objects and other objects.

Demonstrate relationships of objects by using blocks, toys and classroom equipment. Let children carelessly toss blocks into a box, then remove them. Count the number of blocks the box held. Next let them carefully stack the blocks into the box, fitting them close together. Add more blocks until the box is as full as before. Remove the blocks and count them. Did the box hold more or less blocks when they were carelessly stacked in it?

Set up other situations in the room and let children discover spatial and relational concepts. Provide a box and objects of assorted shapes. Ask children to decide how many objects the box will hold and let them prove or disprove the correctness of their judgments.

Draw a square on paper. Provide square, triangular and diamond-shaped pieces of puzzle that fit together. Scatter the puzzle pieces about and ask the children to look at them. Can all the puzzle pieces be put inside the square without arranging them in order? (They will discover that the only way to pile all the pieces of the puzzle inside the square without putting them in order is to pile them *upon* each other; thus they take up space *above* the square.)

Ask other children to arrange the puzzle pieces on the square in order and draw their own conclusions about the space used. *Stack* five books in one spot on the table. *Spread* five books of similar sizes on the table. The children will see that books in a stack, which use space *above* the table, take up less room than the same number and size of books spread *on* the table.

27. Play a Game of Do As I Say

When this game is first played, the teacher should call the directions. After it has been played once the children can take turns calling directions. Only a few children should play at one time.

Some typical directions:

Touch some object *above* your head.
Touch an object *beside* you.
Touch an object *below* you.
Put your hands *around* some object.
Put one hand *inside* an object.
Stand *between* the piano and the door.
Move two chairs *together*.
Move two chairs *apart*.
Make a crayon line *along* the edge of this paper.
Move these chairs *around* the table.
Pick up a *heavy* object.
Pick up a *soft* object in your hand and squeeze it.
Raise your *right* hand.
Raise your *left* hand.
Clasp your hands and hold them *between* your knees.
Stand *along* the wall *beyond* that table.
Go to the calendar and touch any numeral that comes *before* 9.
Touch a numeral that comes *after* 7. Touch a numeral *above* the 10.
Pick up a *thick* book.
Place a *thin* book *between* the *thick* book and the table.

chapter seven

11 Exciting Nature Projects That Teach Kindergartners How to Discover and Enjoy the World Around Them

These nature activities and projects are not presented in the same way as the other activities in this book. Instead the material is of a general, informative nature and class participation results in projects *after* the children have learned the subject material.

The author is aware that teaching about nature's creatures is sometimes very difficult for the teacher in the city, where there are few animals, insects etc. or for the teacher who has had no opportunity to personally study nature's interesting creatures. The eleven discussion and learning projects in this chapter are presented *primarily for the teacher's use.* He or she can choose the best ways to present them to kindergartners.

Teaching nature material to young children is very rewarding. They love to collect specimens, look at nature books, bring in nature pictures, take nature walks, listen for the sounds that creatures make, and observe their natural world.

1. Insects That Jump and Sing

Katydid: The songs of katydids can be heard in the evening in the eastern part of the U. S. (locate on map). These songs are made only by the males. They have *rasps* and *ridges* at the bases of their outer wings. When the males rub these rasps and ridges together, they produce the songs. This rasping sound is the familiar "Katydid, Katydid" that people hear. A male must be full-grown to make his music. This usually does not happen until the end of summer.

The female katydid has a long *ovipositor.* In the early fall she uses this to place eggs on the bark of trees or twigs. She may lay 100 to 150 eggs. The next spring the young katydids hatch. They look much like the adults, but have no wings and are smaller and lighter in color.

In the southern states katydids will have two broods (or families) each season. In the northern states they have only one brood.

Katydids belong to the grasshopper family of insects. They have long antennae. Adult katydids are usually one inch to one and one-half inches in length. Most katydids are green in color, but brown and pink ones have been seen. They live in cherry trees or maple trees and feed on their leaves.

New words to discuss: rasps, ridges, bases, produce, ovipositor, broods, lighter, season, antennae.

Cricket: Crickets belong to the same insect family as katydids and grasshoppers. They do not bite or sting. They have leathery top wings and soft, folded underwings.

The common black or brown cricket can be found living in houses, garages, or under rocks. Some crickets live in houses all winter but most of them die in the fall.

The females deposit their eggs in the ground in the fall and the eggs hatch late in the spring.

When a cricket sings it raises its wings. It has strong hind leg muscles and a lightweight body, so a cricket is a good jumper.

In China, long ago, crickets were caught and kept in cages or in gourds. They were fed bits of lettuce, bits of fish, dead mosquitos, a bit of honey and bits of melons. The people enjoyed hearing the crickets sing.

New words to understand and remember: leathery, deposit, hind, lightweight, gourds.

Crickets Make Good Classroom Pets

In warm weather field crickets can be found during the day under stones or logs. Females can be recognized by their long ovipositors. Pet crickets can be kept in large, rather flat glass bowls or containers. Cover the bottom of the container with an inch layer of gravel for drainage. Cover the gravel with two inches of soil. Cover the container with gauze or fine-mesh screen wire. Keep it out of direct sunlight.

Feed the pet crickets with dry bran mixed with powdered milk, or dry rolled oats. This food should be kept in a small dish in the container. Crickets may also have bits of melon, lettuce, apple or carrot. A bit of bone meal or dog biscuit should also be provided. Put a small container of water in the cricket bowl.

Kindergartners will enjoy watching these pets and listening to their songs.

Grasshopper: Grasshoppers make music but it is not as pretty to listen to as the music made by katydids or crickets. One particular kind of grasshopper sings one song in the daytime and another song at night. Some grasshoppers move about while singing, while others sit still. This "singing" noise is made when grasshoppers rub the *files* of their back legs across the ridges of their wings. Some grasshoppers sing together in a kind of chorus.

The most commonly seen grasshopper is brightly patterned and grows to be about two inches in length.

A female grasshopper thrusts part of her abdomen into the ground when she is ready to lay her eggs. She lays from 20 to 100 eggs and covers them with dirt.

Grasshopper babies look much like their parents, but have no wings. As they grow in size they develop wings.

A grasshopper uses its strong hind legs for jumping. It can jump many times its own length.

Words to learn and use: files, ridges, chorus, abdomen, develop.

Grasshoppers Make Good Pets in the Classroom

Because they are found in the city as well as in the country, grasshoppers are familiar to most young children. They are easy to catch. Encourage children to bring live specimens to school for observation.

A large glass jar or fishbowl makes a good grasshopper

cage. Put at least two inches of dirt in the cage. Egg-laying females may deposit their eggs while in the cage. The top of the cage should be covered with fine screen wire or gauze. Provide a small container of water for these pets and fresh leaves every day. Grasshoppers eat some solid foods too, as crickets do.

2. Some Beetles Children Like

Ladybird Beetles: There are about 350 kinds of ladybird beetles found in the United States. Some people call them *ladybugs,* or just plain *ladybirds.* Most of these 350 kinds are friends of man, but a few, which eat his plants, are his enemies. Man's ladybird beetle friends help him by eating other insects and they eat larvae that do great harm to his crops.

All ladybirds are small. Some are as tiny as the head of a pin. Even these tiny ones find smaller insects and mites to eat. Adult ladybird beetles are oval-shaped and are about one-third of an inch long. (Show on a ruler.) They are bright orange, red, or yellow-orange in color.

All ladybird beetles do not have the same number of spots on their backs (or wing covers). The two-spotted ladybird is found in the United States. Others found here have nine spots, or fifteen spots. Another ladybird beetle, which is found all over the United States and Canada, has six spots on *each* wing cover. Sometimes, when cold weather comes, these ladybirds are found by the thousands in the mountains. Their very short legs and their bright, gay colors make them easy to see.

FIGURE 7-1 HEAD OF STAG BEETLE

The Stag Beetle: The stag beetle gets its name from the males, which have *mandibles* (chewing mouth parts, or jaws) that are quite long and are shaped somewhat like the horns of a stag. (See Figure 7-1)

Children find stag beetles around street or porch lights in the summer. They sometimes call them *pinching* bugs. They can be found on the tops of logs or the sides of stumps. The babies, or *larvae,* of stag beetles are large, white *grubs.* They eat rotting logs or stumps.

Stag beetles are brown or black in color. Only the males have the mandibles, which look like antlers. These mandibles are often as long as the rest of the beetle's body. A stag beetle cannot pinch if it is picked up across the wings with the thumb and forefinger.

Words to learn and use: ladybird, ladybug, larvae, crops, adult, stag, mandible, grub, rotting, stump, antlers.

3. Flies That Really Aren't Flies!

Dragonfly: Dragonflies are flying insects that are familiar to many children. They look like tiny, beautiful airplanes.

There are about 300 kinds of dragonflies in the United States. Some common names for them are *darning needles, stingers* or *mosquito hawks.* Dragonflies are from one to three and one-half inches in length. Their wings have patches of black, brown, blue or red on them in beautiful designs. Dragonflies have quite large eyes that almost cover their heads. They seem to be all eyes!

A dragonfly (which is not really a fly at all) eats insects and gnats and is a very helpful insect. It has a basketlike place on its legs in which it catches its food. Very small insects are eaten as it flies, but when larger insects are caught, the dragonfly will settle on some spot to eat its prey.

Dragonflies are most often seen near bodies of water or in meadows where there is moist ground.

Darning Needles are big, three-inch dragonflies. They have green and blue bodies and lovely, lacelike wings. They are found around ponds and streams.

The *Ten Spot* is a smaller dragonfly with brown-spotted wings.

The *Damselfly* is about two inches in length. The males and the females are colored differently. The male of one species, the *Ruby Spot,* has a red spot at the base of each wing; the female does not. The male *Black-winged Damselfly* has black wings, but the female has dark grey wings with a white spot on each.

Dragonflies and *Damselflies* are easy to tell apart. The dragonfly keeps its wings outstretched when it rests on an object or a plant. The damselfly rests with its wings closed.

Some new words to understand and learn to use: transparent, delicate, veins, patches, designs, prey, outstretched, moist, lacelike, species.

Discuss these questions: Why are these creatures called flies? What does a darning needle look like? Why would people call a dragonfly a darning needle?

Ask children to bring in live specimens of dragonflies, damselflies or both, if possible. Watch them as they alight. How can a child tell the difference between a dragonfly and a damselfly?

Fireflies: Fireflies are often called "lightning bugs." They make a light on the underside of their abdomens. On summer evenings they fly about in the city and in the country, over ponds, swamps and other places, blinking their "taillights" on and off. Children love to chase them and catch them. Holding a few fireflies in one's hand is like holding tiny, blinking Christmas tree lights, or a bit of magic. If many fireflies are placed in a jar there will be almost continuous light.

A firefly is not a fly at all, but a soft-bodied beetle. The females lay their eggs in or on the ground. When the eggs hatch the larvae (babies) eat rotted wood or rubbish. It takes a firefly baby from one to two years to develop into an adult firefly. When a firefly is grown it is about a half-inch in length.

Sometimes children will see wingless fireflies. These are the females of a certain species of fireflies, and are called *glow-*

worms. The female glowworms give off a clear green light. The males have wings but do not give off light.

Fireflies are usually active at night and rest on plant leaves in the daytime. There are about 50 different kinds of fireflies in the United States.

Words to discuss and use: abdomen, underside, continuous, larvae, rotted, wingless.

Mayfly: Mayflies travel in swarms. In the late afternoon or evening in the summer, swarms of mayflies can be seen over or near rivers or lakes. They can be a bother to people because there are so many of them.

Most kinds of mayflies live for only a few hours, but a few may live for a day or more. They have transparent wings. Sometimes campers or people who live near rivers or lakes may be surrounded by mayflies, which get on their clothes, in their food and everywhere. Fortunately they do not bite and in the morning, after being annoyed by swarms of mayflies, people get up to find dead mayflies around the camp or cottage.

Note: Make sure children understand the meanings of words such as swarms, surrounded and annoyed.

4. How to Tell Butterflies and Moths Apart

Flying Habits. Butterflies fly in the daytime. They seem to prefer sunshine. If the days are cloudy, butterflies will rest on twigs or bushes. Few butterflies are seen after the sun goes down.

Most moths hide in the daytime. When darkness approaches they begin to fly. Many of them seem to be attracted by bright street lights. They can often be seen fluttering around them. Large moths often fly against the screens or window panes of lighted rooms, as if trying to reach the lights inside.

The time of flying is not always a true way to tell the difference between butterflies and moths, however. A few butterflies have been seen flying at night and moths have been seen fluttering in the afternoon sunshine. Their flying habits are a fairly accurate way to tell them apart.

FIGURE 7-2
MOTH BODY WITH FEATHERY ANTENNAE

FIGURE 7-3
MOTH BODY WITH SLENDER ANTENNAE

FIGURE 7-4
BUTTERFLY BODY

FIGURE 7-5
BUTTERFLY ANTENNAE

FIGURE 7-6
MOTH ANTENNAE

Body Shapes. Moths usually have heavy, full bodies and their heads are small and hard to see. (See Figures 7-2 and 7-3) Butterflies have slender bodies, with easily seen heads. (See Figure 7-4)

The antennae of butterflies have knobs or little clubs at the ends. (See Figure 7-5) The antennae of moths may be feathery, slender, or look like little plumes. The antennae of males and females differ. (See Figure 7-6)

Cocoons or Chrysalises? Most butterfly caterpillars make chrysalises in which to spend their pupa stage of development.

Most moth caterpillars spin cocoons for themselves. A few, like the tomato caterpillar, burrow into the soil and spend the pupa stage there.

Wings. A moth holds its wings down flat over its sides and back. A butterfly holds its wings pointed up over its back.

Suggested Activities: Look at books and pictures of moths and butterflies. Talk about the shapes of their bodies and of their antennae. Examine specimens of real moths and butterflies, if possible. Exhibit pictures of large and small kinds.

Show children how to fold construction paper in half, draw a butterfly shape on one side, cut through both sides of paper and open. Color or paint beautiful designs on both sides of the paper. Suspend these colorful butterflies or moths around the classroom or make mobiles with them.

Provide construction paper and vivid colors in poster paints. Large paintbrushes or small sponges are also needed. Show kindergartners how to fold a 9" x 12" sheet of construction paper. Open it with the folded edge against the table. Use a brush or sponge and apply poster paint to only one side of the folded paper. Fold the dry side of the paper over the painted side. Press together gently. When opened there will be a lovely, vivid, multicolored design. This design can be cut into the shape of a butterfly by letting the paper dry, then cutting it, folded, into the required shape. After experimenting a few times, children will learn to put the paint on one side of the paper in the shape of a butterfly, which will then reproduce its shape when folded.

When thoroughly dry these butterfly designs may be refolded and painted on the other side of the paper. Bodies should be put on them along the fold of the paper using black or brown crayon. Paste on strips of black or brown paper for antennae. Remind the children to put correctly shaped antennae on their creatures so they can be identified.

5. Curious, Creepy, Crawly Creatures!

Interesting facts to talk about and remember:

An insect is an animal with six legs.

An insect often has four wings but some insects, like the housefly, have only two wings.

An insect has *antennae* or *feelers*.

A spider is not an insect because it has eight legs.

A centipede is not an insect. It has about 30 legs.

There are almost a million kinds of insects in the world.

There are more insects in the world than *all* other kinds of animals.

All *bugs* are insects, but not all insects are bugs.

Stinkbugs and giant waterbugs are *true* bugs.

Beetles are the most common insect.

Ants are insects. They are found in very cold arctic regions and in very hot tropical regions. Some kinds of ants are an inch long. Some ants are so tiny that they are hard to see without a magnifying glass.

Lightning bugs are really fireflies.

Lightning bugs aren't bugs and they aren't flies, either. They are really beetles with soft bodies.

Ladybugs are really *ladybird beetles.* Some have two spots, some have six spots, some have nine or more spots.

A grasshopper can jump many times its own length.

A housefly has suction pads on the bottoms of its "feet" so it can climb windows and walk on ceilings.

Honeybees have rear legs that can puff up into "baskets" in which they can store and carry pollen.

Leaf-eating beetles have two kinds of mouth parts, like a built-in knife and spoon. One part cuts their food, the other part spoons it into their mouths.

Moths and butterflies have long, *coiled tubes,* which they can extend like soda straws and suck up flower nectar and plant juices.

A mosquito has a mouth-part that has tiny sharp points that it uses to prick (or cut) a person's skin. The mosquito then makes an opening to insert its sucking tube. When this cut is made, a person feels the mosquito's bite.

Only the female mosquito sucks blood. The males eat plant juices.

A dragonfly uses its legs to make a kind of basket with which it catches insects.

6. Insects, Birds, Animals, and Reptiles That Hibernate
Insects, Animals and Fish That Migrate

To hibernate means "to winter." In the fall, animals, birds and insects that hibernate find a protected place of safety. There they stay all winter without eating or drinking. Their dormant state is best understood by children as a *very deep sleep.*

The word *migrate* means "to wander." Insects, birds and animals that migrate southward in the fall often travel great distances to find more pleasant places in which to spend the winter.

Creatures that *hibernate*
Find quiet dark places
And *hide!*
Creatures that *migrate*
Travel long distances
To *abide!*
Those creatures that hibernate
Are *stay-at-homes.*
Those creatures that migrate
Look for *new homes.*

Hibernation

Insects. Insects cannot fly when the air temperature is below 50°F. Some insects in the northern states hibernate in protected places to survive the cold winter. Those that do not hibernate must die.

Many plant-eating bugs hibernate in the mud at the bottoms of ponds. The adults emerge in the spring and lay their eggs.

Woolly-bear caterpillars hibernate. Mourning Cloak and Red Admiral butterflies hibernate as adults. They hide between rocks or in hollow trees. Sometimes the Red Admiral will spend the winter as a pupa, snug and warm in its chrysalis.

The Painted Lady, the Anglewings and Buckeye butterflies all hibernate in the winter as adults. They appear earlier in the spring than those butterflies that must emerge from chrysalises.

Ladybirds (ladybugs) hibernate, often in vividly colored clusters. Queen wasps hibernate in tree bark or in some buildings. Queen bumblebees also hibernate. In the spring the queen flies about hunting for an empty hole in which to start housekeeping.

Birds. Chimney swifts and hummingbirds hibernate in the winter. When cold weather comes they find a warm, protected place in which to remain until spring.

Animals. Animals that truly hibernate are the bat, woodchuck, dormouse and groundhog. Bears, raccoons, foxes and other small animals become inactive in the winter, but they do not truly hibernate. They occasionally emerge from their warm homes to feed.

Reptiles. Not all reptiles hibernate, but some snakes, lizards, newts and turtles will bury themselves in mud when the air becomes cold. They remain there all winter.

Migration

Insects. Swarms of butterflies migrate in the spring and fall. Most children, even in the city, are familiar with the Monarch butterfly. It is famous for its migration to Pacific Grove in California. Monarchs are strong fliers. Once a Monarch was banded in Canada and later was seen at a place in Mexico, a distance of over 1,800 miles.

Other butterflies that migrate are the Painted Lady and some of the Sulfurs.

Groups of dragonflies have been seen flying southwest in the fall. Swarms of dragonflies move from one place to another, perhaps in search of mosquitos. They devour mosquitos in great quantities and do man a service in helping to lessen the numbers of these pests.

Animals. Caribou herds, which live in arctic regions in the summer, migrate south in the late fall. Some herds of deer and moose have been seen in the fall moving south to protected areas where they can find abundant food.

Fish. Fish constantly "wander" or migrate from place to place in search of food, but little is known about how far they travel. The "walking catfish" in Florida has been observed migrating on land.

Things to do: Make sure that children understand the meanings of *hibernate* and *migrate.* Discuss other words that are new to them. Display pictures of migrating Monarch butterflies, if possible. Show pictures of hibernating turtles and other small creatures. Old and obsolete school textbooks are excellent sources of such pictures.

7. Snails and Where to Find Them

Garden snails (See Figure 7-7) are small creatures with bodies shaped like the horns of a male sheep. They are brown in color with a small body that comes out of the shell and leaves a trail of sticky secretion behind it as it moves along. This snail has an operculum (or door), which it closes behind it as it retreats into its shell for safety.

Land snails (see Figure 7-8) like to eat plants. They use a gill for breathing.

Fresh-water snails. The winkle snail (see Figure 7-9), the ramshorn snail (see Figure 7-10) and the giant pond snail (see Figure 7-11) are all fresh-water snails found in ponds and lakes. There is also a dwarf pond snail, not pictured, which is shaped like the giant pond snail. These snails must come up for air now and then. They have a lung and a gill. These snails can move along the glass of an aquarium by means of a broad, muscular foot. (See Figure 7-12)

Salt-water snails have many shapes all of which somewhat resemble the pictured fresh-water snails. The Pomacea snail,

FIGURE 7-7 GARDEN SNAIL
WITH CLOSED OPERCULUM

FIGURE 7-13 POMACEA SNAIL
WITH CLOSED OPERCULUM

FIGURE 7-8 LAND SNAIL

FIGURE 7-9 WINKLE WITH FOOT

FIGURE 7-10 RAMSHORN WITH FOOT

FIGURE 7-14 TREE SNAILS

FIGURE 7-11 GIANT POND SNAIL

WITH FOOT ON GLASS OF FISHBOWL

ON SANDY BOTTOM

FIGURE 7-12 FRESH-WATER SNAIL

which is common to marshes in South Florida, is the *only* food eaten by the rare Everglades Kite. (See Figure 7-13)

Tree snails are bright, beautiful, striped creatures that live in trees. They feed on bark and leaves. (See Figure 7-14) These snails attach themselves to trees in the dry season. A gluelike substance excreted from their bodies holds them there. They become inactive. When the rainy season comes the substance softens and the snail moves about again. It might be said that these snails *hibernate* in their own shells not because of cold weather, but because of dry weather.

New words to understand and use: operculum, retreat, gill.

Things to do: Put some fresh-water snails in a fishbowl. These snails may be found by children in ponds and lakes. They are inexpensive to buy at a pet shop. Kindergartners enjoy watching snails move about in a fishbowl. If snails are kept in a tank without fish, which gobble up the eggs, the snail eggs will hatch. There will be an exploding population of tiny snails for children to enjoy.

8. Who-o-o Knows About Owls?

What are owls? Owls, in general, are birds with large heads and eyes, odd-looking faces with sharp beaks, chunky bodies and sharp claws or talons. Most of them hunt at night. They make very little noise as they hunt because the soft edges of their wings muffle the sound of the wingbeats.

An owl's eyes are fixed in their sockets and do not move but seem to stare. The iris can be expanded so it can use every bit of light in the nighttime. An owl's iris contracts in the daytime, but owls can see quite well by day.

There are eighteen different kinds of owls in North America. The most interesting of these are the great white owl of arctic regions; the great horned owl; the barn owl, which is familiar to many children; the screech owl; and the tiny elf owl of the southwest, which is not much bigger than an English sparrow.

Owls eat crickets, cutworms, grasshoppers, beetles, katydids, moths, caterpillars, mice, moles, bats, snails, crayfish, spiders, small animals and small birds. Adult owls use their feet and talons to seize and kill their prey.

Barn owls are found in almost every country in the world. There are many different kinds. The ones seen in the United States are tan and white in color. These owls are rather large. Adult birds may grow from twelve to nineteen inches in length. They never migrate but live in the same region both summer and winter.

These large barn owls are very valuable to farmers. Rats and mice, which eat the farmer's grain, are the main food of these birds. They live in barns, of course, but barn owls also live in church belfries or abandoned houses. They can hunt in darkness for they hunt by sound and not by sight.

The females lay from five to seven eggs early in the spring. In about a month the eggs hatch. The baby owls learn to fly when they are two months old. Barn owls are often called *feathered flying mousetraps.* (See Figure 7-15)

The *screech owl* is the most familiar owl in the United States. It is the only small owl that has ear tufts. Screech owls are sometimes reddish brown and sometimes grey in color. They are found in the woods, in orchards, on farms and in towns. They like to make their homes in tree holes, but they have been known to move into large birdhouses with sawdust on the floor.

A screech owl will eat moths, frogs, small birds, bats and so on. They are very courageous about protecting their nests.

Many children have heard the plaintive cry of the screech owl. It is quite different from the calls of other owls. (See Figure 7-16)

The *tiny elf owl* is no bigger than an English sparrow. It lives in the dry desert regions of the southwestern states. It doesn't build a nest; instead the elf owl searches for an old abandoned woodpecker hole high up in a cactus plant.

The little elf is sometimes hard to see for it looks like its surroundings. There are touches of yellow, white and grey among its brown feathers. Its big eyes are yellow in color. It has a short tail, just one-half the length of one wing.

From two to five eggs are laid by the female. Both parents take care of the white eggs. The chicks, when hatched, are only two inches tall and are covered with snowy white down.

This small owl never comes out of its nest in the daytime. At night it hunts for grasshoppers, ants, beetles and other creatures.

Elf owls call to each other with a chattering sound, but few people ever hear them. (See Figure 7-17)

The *great horned owl* is the fiercest and most savage of all owls. It grows to be from eighteen to twenty-five inches in length. It is a beautiful wild bird and is the largest of our tufted owls.

Although the great horned owl eats insects, wild birds, snakes and wild game birds, it has been known to catch cats, skunks and even smaller owls.

These large owls do not build their own nests. They use the abandoned nests of other large birds. (See Figure 7-18)

The *snowy owl* lives in the northland, but sometimes migrates to the United States and Canada in the winter time. It is equal in size to the great horned owl and is a large, white, beautiful bird.

Most owls hunt and feed at night, but in the arctic regions, because there is darkness for long periods of time then light for long periods, the snowy owl has learned to hunt in the light. These owls are easy to see along lake shores and along the seacoast. Many of these beautiful owls are shot in winter by hunters who want them for trophies. (See Figure 7-19)

Things to do. Discuss these words so children will understand them: muffle, iris, contracts, tufts, abandoned, surroundings, game birds, belfries, trophies.

Ask children to answer these questions:

Why is a barn owl called a feathered flying mousetrap?
Why is the tiny elf owl given that name?
Do elf owls talk to each other?
What is the largest of our tufted owls?
Would it be possible to see a snowy owl without traveling to the arctic regions? How?

9. City Pigeons

Pigeons live in both the country and the city. They were first brought to this country by the early settlers. In those days they were used for food. They were used to carry messages

FIGURE 7-15
FACE OF BARN OWL

FIGURE 7-18
HEAD OF GREAT HORNED OWL

FIGURE 7-16
SCREECH OWL

FIGURE 7-19
HEAD OF SNOWY OWL

FIGURE 7-17
TINY ELF OWL

from place to place. Some people also trained pigeons as racing birds.

Many city people enjoy pigeons because of their tameness, their beauty and their soft cooing. Other people do not like the dirt they make on buildings.

In the cities pigeons make their homes in public buildings, along ledges, even in attics when they find holes to enter. They will nest in any spot where they can be sheltered from the weather. They gather in the city parks, where people like to feed them. They find much food in the streets and alleys.

Pigeons choose just one mate and they make their home together for the rest of their lives. When they make a nest the male collects the nesting material. He takes one straw or one twig at a time to the female. She places it in a very careless pile, which does not resemble the neatly shaped nests of many birds. The female pigeon lays two eggs. Both male and female warm the eggs, taking turns.

Baby pigeons are called *squabs.* They are fed a very strange food called *pigeon's milk.* Only members of the pigeon family can produce this kind of food for their babies. The pigeon's milk is white in color and is similar to real milk. *Both* parents have this milk in their crops. The squabs put their bills into their parents' bills and there they are fed. As they grow older there are other kinds of food mixed with the pigeon's milk in their parent's crop.

When the babies are three or four weeks old they leave the nest. The father pigeon shows them food on the ground. Soon they are looking for their own food.

Pigeons raise as many as five families a year. A pigeon has been known to live thirty or more years. Since they raise two babies at a time and sometimes raise ten babies every year, soon there could be as many pigeons in a city as people.

Many people in the city cannot have other kinds of pets such as dogs and cats in their apartments because their landlords have rules against pets. These people make pets of the city pigeons. They feed them on their window sills and in the parks. A city without pigeons would be an unusual place.

Things to do. Make sure that the children understand and

can use these words: attics, ledges, sheltered, careless, resemble, squabs, pigeon's milk, crops, unusual, similar.

Some questions to discuss:

Does a male pigeon choose a new mate every year? [no]
What is a baby pigeon called? [squab]
What is a crop? [in birds the crop is the place where food is partially digested]
How many eggs does a female pigeon lay at one time? [2]
How many families do a pair of pigeons raise each year? [4 or 5]
How many babies can a pair of pigeons have in one year? [8 or 10]
Do *all* people in the cities like pigeons? [no] Why?

A Finger Play

(Children bend to the floor as their fingers become fluttering pigeons)

Ten pretty pigeons,
Sit in the sun,
On a church roof,
When day is done.
Ten pretty pigeons,
Flutter down,
To pick at bread crumbs,
Scattered around.
Five pretty pigeons,
Flutter aloof,
Then five more pigeons,
Fly to the roof.

10. Ears and Eyes Grow in Strange Places and in Strange Ways

Ears. Where are a frog's ears? A frog's ears are hard to find. The big circles in back of a frog's eyes are its ears.

Are a grasshopper's ears on its head? A grasshopper's ears are under its wings.

Owls' ears. Some owls have a tuft of feathers on each side of their heads. Other owls have no feather tufts on their heads. *Are the feather tufts ears?* If an owl is without feather tufts, is it also without ears? An owl's tufts are not ears, but bunches of feathers. An owl's ears are on each side of its head, but they are hidden by its feathers.

Whales do not have ears on the outside of their bodies. They have sensitive hearing canals inside their bodies.

Eyes. A *starfish* has one eyespot at the tip of each arm. As the starfish climbs around on rocks in search of food, his many eyes tell him where to find it.

A *crayfish* has two enormous eyes and they swivel around, so it can look in all directions.

A *turtle's* eyes look downward, so it can see what it is eating.

A *toad's* eyes stick up above its head. It can bury itself in the soil with its head covered, but it can still see all around with its protruding eyes.

The *crab spider,* which is usually yellow and lives in goldenrod blossoms, has eight eyes on its head.

A *flounder* fish has both of its eyes on the same side of its head unlike other fish whose eyes are placed with one eye on either side of their heads. A flounder lies on its side at the bottom of the ocean. An eye on that bottom side would be useless. Nature arranged that the flounder, when a tiny fish, could move its eye on the underneath side of its body up to the top side of its body beside the other eye.

The *grasshopper* has two large eyes and several smaller eyes on its head.

An *owl's* eyes do not move and the owl must turn its head to see in different directions.

The *ostrich* has larger eyes than any other animal in the world including the elephant, hippopotamus or rhinoceros.

Activity: Discuss the location of peoples' eyes. They use both eyes to look in the same direction. Where are a bird's eyes located? Talk about the eyes and ears of furry and feathered creatures that kindergartners know well. Where are the eyes placed? Are the ears large or small? Are they placed in the same ways on all the animals? Can an animal with large ears hear better than one with small ears?

Ask children to cover one eye, then look around them. Can they see as well with one eye closed as they can with both eyes open? Let them discuss what happens to their vision when one eye is closed.

Make sounds of various kinds and ask children to listen to them with both ears; cover one ear and listen; cover the other ear and listen to the sounds. Make a chart about interesting facts the children have discovered about their ears and their hearing.

11. Animals Left Over from Prehistoric Times

The Musk Ox. The musk ox is a very interesting animal that goes back to the Ice Age and is truly a leftover from prehistoric times. At certain times of the year it lives as near to the North Pole as 380 miles. Most people have never seen a musk ox.

This large animal has a huge, shaggy head like that of the bison and looks toward the ground as a bison does. It has a hump on its back, long, heavy, shaggy hair that hangs almost to the ground, curving horns and short legs with cloven hooves. Although it may look ferocious and dangerous to man, the musk ox is a friendly and gentle animal. It feeds on plants, berries and mosses, green or frozen.

This animal gets its name from the scent glands it has below each eye. When the animal is in danger from its enemy the white wolf, it rubs its head against its front legs. The powerful scent it gives out from its scent glands is called musk. This scent can travel a long way. It arouses the musk ox to charge its enemy. It may also serve to frighten away a nearby enemy.

When a herd of musk oxen are attacked by white wolves, the big animals will form a square with their heads pointing outward. The cows and calves are kept safe inside these squares. A bull may leave the formation to charge a wolf, but he will return to the same place again.

Musk oxen have protective coloring just as many other animals have. Their long, shaggy fur is the color of the rocks where they live much of the time. Their almost-white noses and patches of hair on their foreheads resemble snow on the rocks.

The heavy hair on their bodies keep the animals warm. It also shelters and protects young calves. They get underneath the big bulls and hide from their enemies, the white wolves; or they keep warm and safe from storms.

It is believed that once musk oxen lived in the middle-western part of the United States. Great mammoths and mastodons lived there with them as well as woolly sheep, wolves and other animals. This was the Ice Age, when a great sheet of ice covered Canada and the northern part of the United States. As the air grew warmer the glaciers melted. The mastodons and mammoths died out and their bones and parts of their frozen bodies have been found in the arctic regions. The musk oxen survived and today are still much like those Ice-Age animals.

Things to do. Discuss the words: formation, musk, protective coloring, mammoth, mastodon, arctic regions, refuge.

Locate the arctic region on a globe, map or both.

Discuss the musk oxens' square formation when danger threatens them. Ask a few children to demonstrate such a formation.

> Why are the cows and the calves kept inside the square? Why do the calves sometimes take refuge beneath the bulls?
>
> Is the musk ox a ferocious animal? Does it have any way of telling its enemies to "stay away"?
>
> Why is the musk ox said to be left over from prehistoric times? If you had lived in prehistoric times, would you have seen an animal much like the musk ox of today?
>
> Look at pictures of musk oxen. Compare them with pictures of the American bison and the water buffalo. How are the three animals alike? How do they differ in appearance?
>
> The musk ox is called a musk sheep by some people. Does it look like a sheep?
>
> Name other animals that live in arctic regions. Polar bears can live in zoos. Could a musk ox live in a zoo?

The Blue Whale. The blue whale is the largest living animal on record. One that was captured in 1948 was almost ninety feet long and weighed one hundred fifty tons.

Whales have lived in the sea for many millions of years. Before that they are believed to have walked about on land. They may have gone to the sea to live because they could not find proper food on land. They have now lost the legs they used for movement on land. The front flippers of the blue whale still have five fingerlike projections.

A whale is not a fish, although it lives in the water. It is a mammal and the female feeds her baby with milk from her own body.

Cold does not bother whales because their frames are covered with a layer of blubber or fat. This fat is sometimes twelve inches thick (show on foot ruler.) Whales were once constantly hunted for their blubber. It was food for Eskimos and blubber oil was used by them for fuel. Whales are still hunted, but not in the same ways.

A whale has no outside ears, but it has sensitive hearing canals for use under water. It feeds by opening its mouth wide and taking in a few thousand gallons of water. In this sea water are many creatures that serve as food for the whale. The salt water is not swallowed, but is jettisoned.

When a whale dives into the water it can stay down for almost an hour. Its nostrils close and its lungs expand. As it surfaces for a breath of air, the warm air from the whale's lungs makes a stream of vapor shoot high into the air. This makes a sound that can be heard for some distance.

Things to talk about: How do we know that whales have lived in the sea for millions of years? Why do scientists think that a whale's front flippers were once like feet?

The blue whale is very large. Could children expect to see a blue whale in a city aquarium with other large fish?

Are there small whales in city aquariums? Are these whales *baby* blue whales, or are they full-grown whales of another species?

Is a whale a fish?

chapter eight

22 *Fascinating Science Experiments and Demonstrations*

How Sounds Are Made

Sounds are made by vibrations. Vibration means moving back and forth very rapidly. (Hold a piece of paper and vibrate it to show the children the rapid movement.) When people or animals make sounds it is because the vocal cords in their throats are vibrating. Vibrations may make many kinds of sounds; soft ones, loud, high, low, pleasant or unpleasant ones.

The music on a violin is made by the vibration of the violin strings. Guitars, banjos, harps and ukuleles are other musical instruments with strings. Other instruments have sheets of metal or skin that vibrate such as cymbals and drums.

Sound waves travel through the air like little ripples of water travel along in a brook or river. When a sound is being made nearby people hear it distinctly. If they move away from the object that is making the sound, the sound grows less. If rows of trees or thick curtains are between a person and loud sounds, the sounds are not heard as distinctly. The vibrations that make the noise are stopped by the trees or curtains. (Demonstrate by using a shallow pan, water and a plate or cardboard. Ask a child to blow vigorously on the water to make ripples. Let the children watch as a cardboard or plate is inserted to stop the ripples while they continue to flow at one end of the pan. They will observe that beyond the barrier the water is calm.)

Sounds can travel well through solid ground. In olden days Indians could put an ear to the ground and hear the sounds of riders approaching. They could figure out the nearness of buffalo herds by listening to vibrations in the ground.

1. Activity—Sounds Made by Living Creatures

Ask children to name all the kinds of sounds people make: whisper, yell, scream, cry, hum, sing, murmur, shout and so on. Ask them to name the sounds they have heard animals make. What kinds of sounds do they hear at home? What are the sounds of machinery?

Select a few of these sounds. Ask children to make one sound at a time letting the sound vibrations go out into the room; now, without lessening the sound volume, ask children to tightly cover their mouths. What happens? Experiment with scarves across the mouths or break the sound waves by holding books across the face.

2. Activity—Sounds Made by Musical Instruments

Bring some musical instruments to the room and make sounds with them. Does a drum beaten slowly make more noise than a drum makes when beaten very rapidly?

Strike blocks of wood together. Listen to the sounds. Does the sound grow louder or softer as the speed used to strike the blocks together increases?

Let the children experiment with a stringed instrument, if possible. What happens when the strings are held down with the fingers?

Triangles and cymbals are interesting sound-makers. Encourage children to make a few noise-makers of their own from scrap materials.

3. Activity—Sound Vibrations in the Schoolroom

Provide a blanket or pillow. Let children take turns covering their ears with these objects while loud music is played in the room. The sound vibrations are in the room. Can the children with covered ears hear them? Are they loud? Soft?

If possible put a record player inside a small closet and turn the volume to *loud*. Close the closet door. What has happened to the sound waves? Open the door, then close it halfway. Talk about what is happening to the sound waves from the record player.

Use the record player to listen to voices, then to music, with the volume set at the same place for both. Encourage children to arrive at conclusions about sounds.

What Are Echoes?

When sound waves hit a solid wall they will bounce back. The sound that is bounced back is called an *echo*. Loud words, the sound of wood being chopped, the noise of a motor, a horn blast or the ringing of a bell all can return as echoes if the sound waves hit a solid wall.

Mountains make a very solid wall for sound waves to bounce against. If a person stood on one side of a valley and called loudly across it to mountains on the other side of the valley, the echo would be loud and clear.

A child could stand in a big, empty auditorium or hall facing a solid wall. If he made a loud sound, he could hear its echo. When experimenting with this kind of echo a child should stand as far away from the wall as possible, so the sound of his voice and the echo will not run together.

Gravity

Introduction: The pull of the earth is called *gravity*. The earth pulls everything on it and everything near it. Apples fall from trees to the earth. A ball dropped from a tall building would fall to the earth. Gravity holds people on the earth. If the earth did not have its pull people, animals and buildings would fly out into space. All the air around the earth, which people must breathe, would be gone. All the water from the oceans, rivers, lakes and ponds would run off into space.

Draw a circle to represent the earth. Draw another circle around the first one to show about how far from the earth the pull of gravity extends.

Spacemen and Gravity

Is the moon too far away from the earth to feel the earth's pull of gravity? What happens when our spacemen are on the moon? Must they be careful about how they move? Is there gravity on the moon?

When spacemen are in their spaceships, do they feel the pull of gravity? We know the spacemen float around in their ships without gravity to control their bodies. Try to imagine what it would be like to float around in space.

A man cannot walk on the ceiling of a room. Why? A fly can walk on the ceiling of a room. It has small suction cups on its feet that help it to stick to the ceiling. (Be sure children know how suction cups work. Demonstrate with a child's toy dart.)

The earth pulls each person *with as much force as that person's weight.* If a child weighs forty pounds the earth pulls him with a force of forty pounds. If there were no gravity nobody would weigh anything. How much do spacemen weigh when they travel in space? How much do spacemen weigh when they stand on the moon?

Activity: Weigh each child and record his weight. Make a chart showing the child's name, his weight, and the amount of force with which each child is pulled toward the earth. Keep the chart on display for awhile.

> *Some ideas to think about:*
>
> Would a child weigh as much as he does if there were no gravity?
> Would a child weigh as much as he does if there were *less* gravity than there is now?
> Would a child weigh as much as he does if there were *more* gravity than there is now?
> If there were no gravity, how heavy would an elephant be?
> If there were no gravity could a child lift an elephant?
> Water now runs downhill. If there were no gravity would water run uphill?
> Would water run out of a faucet if there were no gravity?
> Could a man climb a mountain if there were no gravity?

Draw a circle to represent the earth. Let children sketch people, trees, buildings and other objects around the earth as they might look if one could see the earth. Is there ever any danger of objects falling off the earth?

Magnets

Introduction (A Story to Read or Tell)

Long, long ago people were afraid to sail ships in the ocean. Sailors were afraid to go very far from land. Ships often got lost and could not find their way home. Finally somebody learned how to make a *compass*. The needle in the compass always pointed north or south. Sailors could now use the compass because its needle always showed them which way to go. If they knew where north was, they could find south, east and west. They could find their way home when they were out in the ocean with no land in sight.

4. Introduce the Compass

Let the children examine many compasses, if possible. Take them outside the school building and locate north. Ask them to decide if their homes are north of the school. Talk about the directions south, east and west. In which direction do children walk home from school? Does a child walk only in one direction or many directions?

Explain that a compass has a *magnet* in it. (An explanation of the earth's magnetic poles is not needed here.)

5. Introduce Magnets

Provide magnets of many sizes and shapes, if possible: a bar, horseshoe, U-shape, ring, rod and other shapes.

Provide a box of small objects made of iron or steel. Among these objects of metal scatter objects that look as if they are made of metal, but are not. Explain that a magnet will pick up objects only made of iron or steel because it attracts these metals. *Attract* means pull, and the magnet pulls the metal.

Some magnets are stronger than others. A very strong magnet will make pieces of metal jump to it. The size of a magnet does not tell how strong it is for a very small magnet might be very strong.

Magnets are used on big derricks. They pick up scrap iron.

These big magnets are run by electricity. When the electricity is turned off they drop their loads of iron. Magnets run by electricity are called *electromagnets*. Magnets that are magnets all the time are *permanent* or lasting magnets.

6. Experiment—Practical Ways to Use Magnets

Tie strings on magnets. Ask the children to scatter objects on the floor, then pick them up from a standing position.

Drop an iron object behind a large piece of furniture. Pick up the object without moving the furniture.

Drop some pieces of money on the floor. Use the magnets on strings and try to pick up the money.

7. Experiments with Magnets

Place some pieces of paper on the table. Can they be picked up with a magnet? Place a magnet beneath one piece. Can it be picked up at the place where the magnet is? Can the paper be picked up anywhere on its surface? Let children move the magnets about to find out these answers.

Will the magnet attract metal or another magnet through glass? Provide a smooth-edged piece of glass for experimentation.

Will the magnetic pull go through wood?

8. Experiment—Have Fun with Magnets

Make a magnet. Rub a piece of steel across a magnet many times. Always be sure to rub it *in the same direction*. Now try to pick up some paper clips with the *new* steel magnet. Does it work? Let each child have the experience of making a magnet.

Leave magnets and a box of metal and nonmetal objects on a table so children can play with them. Children will discover for themselves that the *poles* of a magnet have a stronger pull that the rest of the magnet.

Cut small fish, all the same size, from gold construction paper. Divide the class into two teams and number the children. Fasten small magnets to the backs of the fish with tape and scatter the fish into two piles, magnet side down. Include many fish without magnets.

Two children will use magnets on strings and "fish," beginning and ending at the same time. The fish are counted and the child who has caught the most fish makes a point for his team. Next the two children numbered 2 will play against each other, the 3's and so on, until all members of each team have played. The team with the most points is the champion team.

Discuss these words and their meanings: monster, compass, needle, devoured, direction, attract, magnetic, pull, equal strength, various, poles, permanent, lasting, electromagnet.

Water

The Importance of Water

All living things must have some water to survive. Some animals can live longer without water than others. A human cannot live without water for more than a few days.

Human bodies are made partly of water. If a child weighed 40 pounds, about 24 pounds of that weight would be water. (Demonstrate by using a piece of paper or a paper figure of a child folded into fifths. Show the children three-fifths to represent the water on human bodies. Show them two-fifths which is not water.) Each day people lose water from their bodies. A person should drink a least six glasses of water a day to replace the water lost.

The water that people drink comes from many places. Country people and people who live in small towns often use water from deep wells in the ground. Sometimes the water is pumped up from the ground with a pump into a bucket. Sometimes the water is piped from a well to faucets inside the house. People also use water from springs, lakes, rivers, and reservoirs. Often water must be brought to cities in pipes or channels called aqueducts. Water may come from great distances. Dams are often built across rivers to make lakes in which water is stored. This water is used by people in the city and in the country.

All water is not fit to drink. Ocean water is too salty. Some water is too muddy; some has a bad taste because of certain minerals in it. Some water looks clear and tastes good, but has disease germs in it that make it unsafe to drink. In most large or small cities the water is made pure enough to drink by filtering it or adding chemicals to it.

9. Experiment—Clean Water Is Important

Experiment with water in which there is sediment. Pour it through a piece of cloth so kindergartners can see the dirt that remains on the cloth. Compare samples of the filtered and the unfiltered water.

10. Activity—Visit a Local Department of Waterworks

Add a small amount of salt to water and let children taste it. Add more salt and let them taste it. Could people drink salty ocean water?

Discuss the local source of water. If possible take the class to visit the local department of waterworks. What is added to the water to make it pure?

Evaporation of Water into the Air

Wipe the chalkboard with a wet sponge. Tell the children to watch the water on the chalkboard disappear. Where has the water gone? Explain about evaporation. Can the water be seen in the air of the classroom? Can it be felt in the air?

When water goes into the air it is called *water vapor*. Water vapor can get into the air in many ways. It evaporates from lakes, rivers and ponds. Water leaves wet clothes when they hang on a line and becomes water vapor.

It the air becomes quite full of water vapor, little drops of water are formed. These are very small drops that stay up in the air as clouds. If the little drops become large and join together, they fall to the earth as rain.

Water Can Be Changed

The water people drink is a liquid. This liquid will run through the fingers; pour out of a cup or glass; spread over a floor or other surface; soak into a cloth, or into the ground. The water used most frequently is in liquid form.

Water can be changed into a *solid* form so it can be held in the hand instead of running out of the hand. This solid is called ice. When water becomes very cold it forms crystals of ice. When moisture in the air, or water vapor, becomes very cold, it forms ice crystals and falls to the ground as snow. Sometimes ice pellets are formed and fall to the ground as hail.

Water can be changed into another form called gas. The *steam* that comes from the spout of a teakettle is in the form of gas. Steam can be made by heating water until it boils.

11. Experiment with Water Solids

If a refrigerator is available, freeze water into cubes. Talk about the solid form of ice. Set some ice cubes or a small block of ice out in the air of the classroom so the warm air will melt them.

Use a hot plate or candle flame to apply heat to other ice cubes. Ask children to discuss the methods of changing solid water to liquid water. Which was quicker—the air-warmed way or the direct-heat way?

12. Experiment—Learn About Steam and Water Vapor

Put some ice cubes or block ice into a teakettle. Apply heat. Children can watch the heat changing the solid water to a liquid. Allow the water to boil. Now they can watch the liquid become a gas as it escapes into the air as *steam*. Can the steam be seen in the air? If the steaming kettle is held near a cold surface, the water vapor will form droplets on the surface as it cools. Is the gas changing back to a liquid? Watch the kettle until all the water has become steam and the kettle is empty. Encourage kindergartners to arrive at conclusions about the steam. Where did it go? Did they smell the steam? Did they see the steam as it left the kettle? Did they see the steam after it became part of the air?

Some questions to stimulate thinking:

Is water that comes out of the faucet always a liquid?
Is water that comes out of a teakettle spout always steam?

There is water vapor in the air. Can you pour water vapor?
What form of water would you find in a deep freeze?
Could water in a deep freeze ever be a liquid?
Is water in a bag of ice always in solid form?

Wind

13. What Is Wind?

Wind is moving air. If there is a mobile in the room, ask several children to stand beneath it and wave their arms back and forth without touching the mobile. It begins to move. There is *wind* around the mobile because the air is moving around it.

Ask children to name several places in the classroom where air can be found. The response will be, "Air is all over," or "Air is all around us!" or "Air is what we breathe."

14. Movement of Air

A child's body can start air movement. Have the class stand, each child a little apart from his neighbor, and let the children start air movement by swaying their bodies. Are they creating a wind? Allow undirected movement while holding two pieces of paper near the children. Is the paper blowing in the wind?

Pass out strips of paper to several children. Ask them to hold the paper by one end, before their mouths, then slowly count to ten. Does the paper move when the child counts? Where is the air, which moves the paper, coming from?

Can wind be seen? Encourage children to discuss this question. Is the wind actually visible or are only the effects of the wind seen? Have them name all of the objects they have seen that cause a wind by making air move: electric fans, paper fans, hairdriers, air conditioners and so on.

Make a list of objects that will move when the wind blows: windmills, leaves, whole trees, a candle flame, a bonfire, etc.

How can wind help people? List all the ways that the kindergartners suggest and add any of the following ways in which wind helps people:

Wind is cool; it dries mother's clothes if she hangs them on the line.
Wind comes out of the registers to keep the house warm.
Wind turns windmills on farms to pump water for animals to drink.
Wind fills the sails of sailboats.
Wind helps kites to fly.
Wind blows seeds from place to place.
Wind blows whole plants here and there.
Wind opens parachutes.

Can wind harm people? Ask children to mention ways in which wind can be harmful. Add these facts to theirs:

Wind can cause bad storms.
Wind can blow shingles from the roofs of houses.
Wind can blow snow into drifts.
Wind can blow down large trees.
Wind can cause high waves that wash away the sand on beaches.
Wind can blow down a farmer's wheat or corn.
Wind can turn umbrellas inside out on a rainy day.
Wind can make fires burn harder and destroy houses.

Can wind be heard? Most children will recall hearing the wind "howling" around a house in a storm. They will have other interesting contributions to make about hearing wind.

Can wind be watched? Wind cannot be seen but children have seen what it *does.* Men's hats blow in the wind, leaves blow against their feet, a maple tree's seeds flutter through the air, a little girl's long hair blows into her eyes. What was the wind blowing around as the children came to school?

Can wind be felt? Can the warm air from a radiator or a hot-air vent be felt? Can a child feel the cool air of a summer evening? In what other ways can the wind be felt?

Does wind have a smell? Has any child ever passed a bakery? Did the warm air coming from that bakery have a smell? When cars are lined up behind each other in a traffic jam, can people smell the fumes from the exhaust? While traveling in the country, has any child ever smelled sweet clover in the fields? Is the smell of pigs a different smell? Are there other smells the wind can bring to a person's nostrils?

Blossoming trees and flowers in the spring have a lovely fragrance. Is their smell carried on the wind? When mother or the teacher wears perfume and comes near a child, can the child smell the perfume? Who moved the air?

15. Flame and Wind

Light a candle. Fan the flame so children can watch the flame begin to burn more brightly. Allow the flame to become small, then fan it to a large glame again. Now explain to the children that fire needs air to burn. Moving air (wind) makes fire burn more rapidly. A flame will die out immediately if covered so air cannot reach it. Use an empty can to cover the burning candle flame. Show children that the flame has stopped burning.

Light the candle again. Ask the children to suggest another way to put out the flame.

16. Wind and Waves

Fill a large shallow pan with water. Let children take turns standing at one end of the pan and blowing on the water to make waves.

Direct an electric fan on the water. Are there larger or smaller waves when there is more air movement?

Questions to ask about wind: Is wind moving air? Can wind help people? Can wind harm people? Do people make use of wind? Are there "wind" machines in homes? Does wind always feel the same on the skin? Can wind be warmed or cooled?

17. Things for Kindergartners to Do When Learning About Wind

Make simple paper fans.

Make simple paper pinwheels and mount them on pencils or dowel sticks.

Make mobiles.

Make wind chimes or clackers from spools, can lids, shells, small mirrors, bits of colored glass, etc.

Use construction paper for an art experience. Put daubs of poster paint on the paper. Let children gently blow the paint on the paper to make designs.

Melt wax crayons. Pour this colorful melted wax on water. Let children blow it into designs.

Kinds of Winds

Children hear adults talk about breezes, high winds, gales, storms, hurricanes, cyclones and tornados. These are simple explanations of terms that often confuse kindergartners:

BREEZES

A *light* breeze:
Is a very gentle movement of air, or wind.
Can be felt on the skin.
Will make a mobile begin to move.
Makes tiny little ripples on water.
Helps clothes to dry on a line.
Moves leaves on trees.
Blows a flag on a flagpole only a little.
Gently blows seeds from place to place.

A *strong* breeze:
Makes big waves and whitecaps on a lake or on an ocean.
Makes dust and paper blow.
Moves branches of trees.
Makes clothes blow on the line.
Blows men's hats from their heads.
Blows leaves from trees.
Makes running or skating hard, if a child goes against the wind.

GALES

A *medium* gale:
Makes large waves.
Breaks twigs from trees.
Makes corn and other grain blow to the ground in the farmer's field.
Piles up snowdrifts in winter.

A *strong* gale:
Uproots trees.
Breaks off great tree branches.
Makes huge waves and foam.
Sometimes blows shingles from roofs; sometimes blows whole roofs from buildings.
Breaks windows.

STORMS

A *storm:*
Blows sleet or snow.
Makes high waves that can overturn small boats.
Can often cause trouble for big boats and ships.

A *tornado:*
Is a violent storm, with violent, whirling winds that destroy
    everything in their path.

A *cyclone:*
Is a tornado or any violent storm.
Is caused by strong, whirling winds.

A *hurricane:*
Is a violent whirlwind.
Is sometimes accompanied by thunder, lightning and rain.
Usually starts out in an ocean.

18. How to Set Up a Moist-temperature Terrarium

A moist-temperature terrarium in which small animals live will delight and fascinate kindergartners. They observe and care for the creatures and acquire knowledge of their needs and habits.

How to begin a *moist-temperature terrarium:* Use a large glass aquarium if several small animals are to share the terrarium with plants. Lay a four and one-half inch layer of sand in the bottom of the container. Over the sand put a one-inch layer of charcoal. This charcoal will provide drainage for the terrarium. Over this lay a two-inch layer of soil in which to plant the desired vegetation.

Clinkers or porous stones are very attractive additions to the terrarium. Small plants can grow around or through these rocks and spread over their surfaces. Build the clinkers or rocks higher at one end of the container for a more decorative effect. The little creatures will climb on them to sun themselves.

Soil for the terrarium should be good garden soil or soil collected from a forest.

Plants may be mosses, ferns, lichens, liverworts, etc., which children can help collect from a wooded area. Ground pines and ferns, if used, should be moved carefully so the roots are not damaged. Stones with lichen or moss growing on them can be moved to the terrarium. Use some decayed dead leaves to mix with the soil for better plant growth.

If soil and wild plants are not available, these materials can be found at a pet store, department store or variety store. Potting soil, charcoal, sphagnum moss and small ferns are desirable. The ferns are planted in the soil. The moss is then pressed into the soil between the ferns and over and around the rocks. Dampen but do not soak the soil.

Glass covers for terrariums are necessary if small animals are to be kept inside. Be sure to allow a way for fresh air to get inside the container. Keep it in a cool location with good light but no *direct* sunshine. Water the soil as a houseplant is watered. With a cover on the terrarium it will probably need to be watered less than once a week.

Keep a small dish of water in the terrarium. A few small stones in the water are necessary. Bigger stones around the water dish will give the little "pool" a decorative touch.

The animals for a terrarium should be selected with care. Frogs and toads, newts and salamanders like the moist-temperature terrarium the best. Small snakes such as garter or green snakes need more sunlight.

Most small turtles can be kept in a terrarium. They need water and dry rocks on which to rest. A turtle needs commercial pet food. He also needs bits of raw beef, snails, earthworms, and bits of fresh vegetables. Some turtles prefer to feed under water, so the water dish may need to be cleaned every day.

Salamanders resemble lizards but do not have claws or scaly skin. Salamanders can be found in damp woods under logs. They must be fed mealworms and *live* insects. For this reason they are more difficult to keep in a kindergarten terrarium.

Newts are a common variety of salamander. When young they are red with spots on them. They live on land and are known as red efts. When full-grown they change color and enjoy life in the water. They breathe air and make good terrarium occupants. They get along with small frogs and toads. Snakes are apt to eat newts.

Toads and peepers (tree frogs) like life in a terrarium. The toads like to be fed insects and a few worms a day. A peeper has "suction cups" on his feet and likes to climb so provide a small branch for him. Frogs and toads want to feed on *moving* food. If the insects they are given are not alive, then they must be tossed to the pets. Their long, sticky tongues flick out and catch the insect in the air.

If frogs are kept in the terrarium, more space must be given to a larger container of water. The water should be filtered, or changed frequently. Under-gravel type filters can be found in pet shops.

The Japanese Red-bellied Salamander and the Eastern United States Newt (Diemyctilus) can both be purchased in pet shops.

19. Kindergartners Love an Aquarium

The size of an aquarium tank should be determined by the number of fish to be kept in the tank. A good rule is one goldfish to a gallon of water; thus five goldfish would be quite comfortable in a five-gallon tank, preferably rectangular in shape.

Fish for the tank can be fancy ones—comets, fantails, telescopes and veiltails. They can be common ones such as gold carp or sticklebacks. Carp are very hardy. Sticklebacks are sticklers to handle but interesting to watch. They build basket-like nests around the stems of water plants.

Plants for the tanks can be of several varieties: Anacharis (or ditch moss) is an excellent outdoor fish pond plant, but will grow a bit large and stringy inside an aquarium unless pinched back now and then. Valisneria (eelgrass) is a decorative plant that grows well. Sagittaria (arrowhead) is said to be an excellent plant for furnishing oxygen to goldfish. Cabomba (fanwort) is also an excellent plant and is a very decorative one. It should *not* be used in a tank with fancy goldfish, however. They will devour it.

Growing plants provide oxygen, food and shelter for aquarium fish. The tank should be kept in partial sunlight for the best plant growth. All of the plants mentioned are usually available at pet shops or in variety or department stores.

Snails for the aquarium are very desirable and necessary. They help to keep the water clean by eating any dead fish or decayed fish food. Snails that will not eat the plants should be used. Buy coral snails or Japanese snails at a pet shop. Ordinary fresh-water snails from ponds may also be used. (See *Snails,* chapter 7.)

If children bring a few fresh-water mussels they will help to keep the aquarium clean.

Sand for the aquarium can be ordinary gravel or colored gravel from a pet shop. Wash *all* gravel or sand until it is quite clean before using it. Cover the fish tank bottom with about two inches of sand. Plant the water plants, making sure that the roots are well spread out in the sand; then cover with another inch of gravel.

Before adding water, cover the plants with a piece of paper. Let the water fall on the paper and it will not stir up the sand. Ordinary pump water or water from the tap can be used. If it is necessary to use boiled water for the tank, pour it out of a sprinkling can, holding the can high above the tank. The water will be aerated when it reaches the aquarium. The water temperature should be kept from 55 to 75 degrees.

An aeration pump to supply plenty of oxygen is excellent for an aquarium. These pumps can be bought at pet stores. Use according to directions.

Children can clean the aquarium themselves. Supply a rubber tube for a siphon. When the water in the tank seems cloudy, remove most of it and replace with fresh water. Have the children fill the siphon with water and hold both ends shut. Provide a large pail to catch the dirty water. Put one end of the siphon into the water and remove the pressure on both ends. The water will run into the pail.

When the sides of the aquarium become green with algae, clean them with a razor blade (in a holder). Wipe the sides clean.

Fresh water should be added after the aquarium is cleaned in the same way as when the aquarium was first set up.

Remind children to feed fish only as much as can be consumed in one day. Uneaten food will decay.

When the aquarium needs a thorough cleaning, use a small dip net and remove the fish to fresh water. Snails may be carefully lifted out with the fingers. Remove the water plants and put aside. Wash the sand or provide fresh sand. Replant the plants and replace the fish and snails. Once more the aquarium is ready for kindergartners to enjoy. They love to watch the fish and become very proficient at keeping the aquarium clean.

20. Growing New Plants in the Classroom

Seedlings. Use a shallow disposable aluminum cake pan or old cake tin. Put a layer of small stones or broken clay-pot pieces in the bottom of the pan to supply drainage. Cover with garden soil, rich loam from the woods, or potting soil. Let children sow tomato, marigold, petunia or other small seeds in the soil. Put the pan in a sunny spot until seedlings are an inch or so in height. Show children how to re-pot the seedlings in paper cups, milk boxes or other small containers.

Cuttings. Purchase vermiculite at a plant shop, department store or variety store. Cover a 6" x 6" disposable aluminum cake pan with two inches of vermiculite. Ask children to bring in begonia or geranium slips or cuttings. Plant them in the vermiculite a few inches apart. When the slips put out small roots, let the children put each plant into its own small clay pot (which kindergartners can usually bring from home).

Plants from "eyes." In a pot plant a potato piece that has several eyes. Soon the potato sprouts will appear. The potato plant will grow into a bushy plant if given sunlight and water.

Tops of vegetables. Cut two inches from the tops of carrots, turnips, beets or parsnips. Put them in a container with pebbles in the bottom. Pour in water so part of the vegetable is submerged. Soon delicate leaves will sprout from the top of the vegetable.

Sweet potato. A lovely sweet potato vine will grow from a sweet potato. Put toothpicks into it at intervals, two or three inches from the top. Suspend the potato in a clear glass or jar of water with the toothpicks resting on the top of the jar. Children enjoy watching new roots appear in the clear water. Soon new leaves sprout at the top of the potato. These sprouts grow into vines which are very decorative.

Citrus plants. Plant orange, lemon or grapefruit seeds in soil for plants with glossy green leaves.

Avocado. Gently peel off the thin outer shell of an avocado pit. Stick a few toothpicks around the outside about ½" from the nonpointed end and suspend this ½" in a glass filled with water. In a few weeks a root will grow and the top will split to allow the plant to sprout. When the plant is a few inches high, pot it in potting soil mixed with vermiculite leaving a bit of the pit showing above the surface of the dirt. An avocado plant will grow tall in a few years to become a showy plant. In eight years it will bear fruit.

21. Grow a Crystal Garden

Children can bring in most of these materials needed for a "crystal" garden:

Rock salt or noniodized table salt
Cake coloring or Easter-egg dye
Clear ammonia
Liquid bluing
Hammer
Brick, coal, or coke
Crockery mixing bowl
Mixing spoon or wooden paint paddle
Eyedropper
Shallow display bowl or disposable 6" x 9" or 9" x 9" aluminum pan

To make: Break the brick or coal into pieces no smaller than walnuts. Put these pieces in the center of the display pan or bowl.

Mix together in order listed:

¼ cup salt
¼ cup bluing
¼ cup water
¼ cup clear ammonia

Pour this solution *slowly* over the pieces of brick, coal, or coke.

Use the eyedropper (or cake-coloring dispenser) and add a few drops of coloring to the pieces.

Set the container in a place of safety, where its contents can be seen but not handled or spilled. Almost immediately some little crystals will start forming. After a few hours the "garden" will have grown all around the inside of the container. The garden will continue to grow for some time. Do not move the container about or shake it. The crystals are very fragile and will crumble.

22. Age and Size Teasers to Talk About

Note: Kindergartners have many wrong conceptions about age, distance, size and so on. These teasers will stimulate discussions and encourage logical thinking.

Age

1. When your baby brother or sister is six months old, is he (or she) young or old?
2. When a grasshopper is six months old, is it young or old? (Old. It is hatched from an egg in the spring and dies that fall, before the weather grows cold.)
3. Is your sister (or brother) old or young when she/he is twelve years old?
4. Is a dog old or young when it is twelve years old? (Old. A dog of 12 is about as old for a dog as a 70-year-old man is for a human).
5. How long do most plants live? (Some for a summer, some bushes and trees much longer.)
6. Could a tree live to be a hundred years old? (Yes, some trees have.) Can a tree live to be three or four thousand years old? (Some of the giant sequoias of California have.)
7. Some kinds of large turtles are called *tortoises.* A giant tortoise can live to be older than an old, old man. Some giant tortoises are not really considered *old* until they have lived for more than 100 years.

Size

8. Is a whale big?
Is an elephant big?
Is an elephant as big as a whale? (An elephant is as big as some kinds of whales. The *blue* whale is much larger than an elephant.

One caught in 1948 weighed 150 tons and that was *3 times more* than the biggest dinosaurs that ever lived. The whale was almost 90 feet long. It would take 20 large elephants to be as big as a blue whale.)

9. Is the earth as big as the sun?
10. Sometimes children catch germs and have diseases. Is a germ big or little? Can you see a germ with your eyes?
11. A polar bear is a huge animal. When full-grown a polar bear could be nine feet long. (Compare this to distances in the classroom.) He could weigh as much as 1,600 pounds. How big is a polar bear *cub* when it is born? (A polar bear cub is about the size of a grown rabbit at birth.)
12. Rabbit mothers have many babies at one time. Usually each one is not more than one inch long. (Show inch on ruler.)
13. A kangaroo mother usually has only one baby. (Never more than two.) Her baby is only one inch long when it is born.
14. Is a rabbit bigger than a kangaroo baby? Discuss. Children will be interested in the comparative sizes of the babies in relation to the sizes of the animal mothers.

chapter nine

25 Tested Approaches That Teach: *Good Manners, Citizenship, Safety, Left from Right, and Relaxing Exercises*

Learning and Using Good Manners

Some kindergartners, when they enter school, have never learned how to live in quiet happiness with other children. They have had no experience with showing concern for the feelings of others, which makes living with other people so much easier and more pleasant.

This learning and using good manners can be acquired by *doing* as children watch their teacher and react to her courteous treatment of them; as they learn the rules of courtesy toward other people and try to follow them; as they become aware of the joy of receiving kindness from their classmates when they give kindness and consideration to others.

What Does It Mean to Have Good Manners?

Discuss the following questions and encourage kindergartners to freely express themselves.

Is it true that other people will be kind to you if you are kind to them?

Do you think you would be happier if every person you know was kind to you?

Would it make you happy to be kind to everybody?

Is kindness good manners?

Is thoughtfulness good manners?

Is making other people happy good manners?

Could the kindergarten room be a happier place if every child was kind and thoughtful? Would you like to learn good manners?

1. Good Manners When Playing with Children

Discuss these schooltime *Do's and Don'ts* with kindergartners and accept their contributions.

Do share toys with other children.

Do take turns when playing with toys and when playing on outdoor equipment.

Do play carefully with toys. They must last a long time and other children want to enjoy them, too.

Do help to put toys away when playtime is over. The classroom is the school-home of all the kindergartners. Help to keep it neat and clean.

Don't push and shove in line.

Don't crowd in ahead of someone else in line.

Don't whine and cry when you can't have your own way.

Give children paper and let each child draw a picture of the Do's and Don'ts that he thinks are the most important. These pictures serve as an excellent insight into a child's self-concept. Some kindergartners feel abused; some feel unloved; others may relate good manners to what they can do to make others happy rather than to what others should do for them.

Display these pictures. The teacher may need to print captions on some of them. Kindergarten pictures are not always self-explanatory!

2. Use Good Manners with Others, at Home, or at School

Always say PLEASE, MAY I? and THANK YOU.

Always ask permission before leaving the table when you have finished eating.

Always use a napkin to wipe soiled hands and mouth at the table.

Always wash your hands before eating.

Always say "Pardon me!" when walking in front of people.

Don't talk with your mouth full of food.

Always wait until another person has finished talking before you speak.

Don't be a butt-in!

Don't yell at people, but speak quietly, in your regular voice.
Don't walk on someone else's feet.
Don't grab things away from other people.
Don't play in other peoples' yards on the way to and from school.
Never pick flowers in the yards of other people.
Never be a litterbug.
Always throw trash in a wastebasket or a trash can.

Ask children to decide on a good-manners rules for them to use in their own homes. These may include:

Don't throw wet towels on the floor.
Don't throw your dirty clothes around.
Don't leave toys where your parents can fall over them! They could get hurt!

Ask children to make a small, *smiling face* at the top of a piece of art paper. Below the smiling face they should draw some ALWAYS pictures.

Another sheet of paper could have a *frowning*, angry face with a turned-down mouth. On it should be pictures of bad behavior which is frowned upon!

3. Good Manners When You Visit a Friend, of Visit Grown-ups

Always remember to be polite to others.
Don't help yourself to food on the table until meal time.
Never open the closed doors of rooms in someone else's house.
Never pull out drawers and look into them.
Never, never carry away a toy that belongs to another person.
Never, never take home anything that was not given to you.

4. Good Manners at the Table, in Your Own Home, and in the Homes You Visit

Never talk with food in your mouth.
Ask for food to be passed to you.
Keep your knife, fork and spoon on your plate after you have used them.
Use a napkin to wipe your fingers and your mouth at the table.
Wait until all the people at the table have been served before you begin to eat.
Don't gobble your food.

Always say PLEASE when you ask for things, and say THANK YOU when you are given things.

5. Good Manners with Pets

Always be kind to pets.
Always make sure that animals have food and water.
Handle pets carefully. Grown-up animals may get angry if you are not kind to them. Baby animals are easily hurt.

Add to these rules if the children feel that more rules are needed.

6. Dramatizations Help Children to Learn Good Manners

Divide the class into groups. Let each group dramatize one of these topics. They may take some Do's and Don'ts and present both good and bad manners; or some groups may want to take only one side and dramatize it. These dramatizations can be done over a period of time. Present one or more to a first grade room if they are good enough to interest other children.

Stress the practice of good manners in the room. Encourage the children to show courtesy to each other and to praise each other. As the teacher practices consideration for her kindergartners, they will find consideration easier for them to practice toward her and toward their classmates.

When the children become very noisy, as they so easily can, get their attention and ask them if they are *all* using good classroom manners. The opinions of his peers are very important to a young child. He *glows* with self-satisfaction when he knows he is behaving well. He loves the approval of his classmates.

Encourage the children to give *honest* and *sincere* praise. Try to establish a positive attitude in the children. Give them, and ask them to give, approval and commendation for *good* behavior and *good* attitudes in their classmates.

7. Have a Party at School

Plan a simple party. Enlist the help of parents and ask for cookies, napkins, paper plates, paper cups, and plastic spoons, if needed.

Children can make paper flowers for centerpieces. They can make place mats, or decorate wide white paper that will be spread on tables.

Show kindergartners how to properly set a table and let them set it.

Ask a few children to pretend to be guests at the party. Ask others to greet them, hang their coats on hangers in the coat room, find chairs for them and make "small talk" until it is time to go to the table.

Choose children to serve the food and others to remove the mats, cups, soiled napkins, etc. from the table when the party is over.

If possible make a recording of the party and take pictures. Kindergartners will love hearing their own voices.

8. A Song to Learn (to the tune of "Mulberry Bush")

Pushers must go
To the end of the line.
Pushers must go
To the end of the line.
Pushers must go
To the end of the line.
Nobody wants pushers *here*.

A Rhyme to Learn

When you meet
Someone you know,
You smile at him,
And say "Hello!"

How to Be a Good Citizen

Introduction: All kindergartners want to be loved and accepted. They need to feel that they *belong* to the group; that they are valued members of a group. How well a child behaves depends on his self-concept. He needs praise from his teacher and his classmates. He needs to know that he can find success in *some* class activities, if not all of them.

In order to feel respect for other children, a child must be shown respect. If good behavior is expected of him, he is more apt to behave well.

Young children need to become conscious of the needs of others. They should learn how to help others.

All of this is citizenship and most young children must be helped to acquire good attitudes and good behavior when they enter school. Discuss with the kindergartners ways in which each child can become a good citizen. Let the kindergartners make their own rules, for they will find their self-made or group-made rules so much easier to follow.

The children may contribute such ideas as:

If someone kicks you, don't kick back!
Don't push a kid's head on the drinking fountain.
Don't crowd in.
Don't throw stuff around.
Don't hit other kids with rocks.
Don't throw dirt in another kid's face.

These rules, while good ones, will have to be revised a bit! The teacher can help the children to set up positive ways in which they can become good citizens at *home,* at *school* and in the *community.*

They will agree to rules like these:

Tell the truth.
Obey school rules so the room will be a happy one.
Work well with other children.
Share with others.
Be a good helper in the room.
Be a good friend.
Listen to directions and do what you are told to do.
Handle books and toys carefully so they will last a long time.
Be kind to others.
Do any task the teacher asks you to do.
Be neat and clean.
Use good manners in the room.
Listen to grown-ups.
Always play fair.
Pick flowers and walk on yards *only* when you have permission.

Touch only those things in houses and stores that you are given permission to touch.

Be brave when you are hurt and frightened. Somebody will help you. Trust policemen.

Obey the patrol boy or girl.

Obey the traffic policeman or woman at the corner when you cross the street.

Help your teacher at school and your parents at home. Wear a happy face!

A Good Citizen Loves His Country and His Flag

Discuss the following rules about the flag:

Keep the flag clean.
Keep the flag from brushing against objects.
Keep the flag off the floor or the ground.
Carry the flag on a pole or a staff.
Do *not* use the flag to decorate clothes.
Boys should remove their hats when they salute the flag.

Safety

When school begins kindergartners should learn good safety rules.

Make *very* large traffic signs and put them on a bulletin board, on a display spot or on a chart. Be sure they are exact duplicates in shape and color, or real signs.

These signs should include: STOP; GO; CAUTION; BUS STOP; CROSSWALK; WALK ONLY ON GREEN; DANGER; and KEEP OFF THE GRASS.

Discuss these signs with children. Some will know many of them.

Talk about the fact that *red* signs mean to *beware, look out* and *be careful.*

9. A Game to Identify Safety and Traffic Signs

Help children to identify the safety and traffic signs by playing an identification game. One child begins the game by holding up a sign-card. He calls the name of the classmate. If that child properly identifies the sign, *he* may hold up the next card.

10. Shapes and Colors of Safety Signs

Give children paper and ask them to make their own safety signs. These may be colored, painted or cut from colored paper and pasted together.

Discuss safety rules that must be observed in the daily lives of children.

11. Some Rules for Walking to and from School

Obey traffic signals and signs.
Walk only on sidewalks.
Always look both ways before crossing streets.
Obey a patrol child at a crossing.
Don't take shortcuts across vacant lots.
Don't walk down dark passageways between buildings.
Don't play in empty buildings.
Don't play in the streets or roads.
Never get into a car with a stranger.
Never accept toys, candy, ice cream or other treats from strangers.
Never play on railroad tracks.
Never play on railroad trestles.
If you must cross a railroad track, look both ways. If a train is coming and the light is flashing, wait patiently on the sidewalk until the train passes.

12. Rules for Bicycle Riding

(These are simple ones, as not too many kindergartners ride bikes to school.)

Never ride a bicycle on the sidewalk among people.
Be careful never to run into another person.
Obey all traffic rules when riding to school.
Never let another child ride with you on the handlebars or any other part of your bicycle.

13. Safety Rules at School

Never stand up on swings.
Never jump out of swings when they are in motion.
Never get off a seesaw without telling your partners.

14. Safety for Children Who Live in the City

Be careful when you walk past construction sites.
Stay away from buildings that are not finished.
Stay away from buildings that are being torn down.
Stay away from holes that are being dug in the ground.
Never play on piles of dirt, rocks or sand.
Never stand near motors when they are running.
Never pick up wires, or touch machinery.

15. Safety Rules for Home

Never play with matches.
Never play around open fires.
Fires can be smothered with rugs, blankets or other objects. (Explain
that fires must have oxygen to burn. Covering a fire will take
away its supply of oxygen and it will go out. Demonstrate this
fact by covering a small paper fire with a can lid or piece of
cloth.)
Stay off high ladders.
Don't climb high trees.
Never throw rocks, knives or other sharp and heavy objects at
anyone.
Never jump from the tops of small buildings.
Never jump out windows.
Be careful when you use kitchen knives, or your parent's tools!
Never leave roller skates where they can be stepped on.
Never leave bicycles or other toys in the driveway, or in the garage,
where they can be run over.

16. A Traffic Light Game

Make a traffic light. Use a tall, narrow box and cut three
holes in one side for the traffic lights.

Insert two round pieces of wood in the box above and
below the light holes. Let them extend from each side of the
box so they can be turned. (Broomstick pieces will do.) On
these rollers put a long strip of paper with red, yellow and green
on it.

Two children may have to turn the rollers. Always show *all*
three lights in one color, red, yellow or green while playing the
game.

Choose a traffic cop. Provide a whistle.

Choose a patrol boy or girl. Make them an identifying badge like that worn by patrol boys and girls in your school.

All the other children in the room are pedestrians. Explain that pedestrians are people who walk from place to place.

Teach the children these rhymes and they must say them as they play the game. They walk on the green light, slow on the yellow light and stop on the red light.

> Green means GO!
> Green means WALK!
> Don't stop to talk.
> The patrol boy says
> "Look both ways
> Before you walk."
> The yellow light means SLOW!
> The green light means GO!
> The red light means STOP!
> Listen to the traffic cop,
> He'll tell you when to SLOW!
> A red light says STOP!
> S T O P !
> Don't run, Don't walk!
> Don't skip! Don't hop!
> Just STOP!

Learning Left from Right

17. Colors Help Children to Learn Left from Right

The teacher will need to show children how to carefully draw around their right hands and to cut out the hand outline. This outline should be cut out of red construction paper, then taped to the child's right hand. (The teacher may have to draw and cut the outline for some kindergartners at the beginning of the year.)

Let the children wear their *red right* hands for several days or until they have become accustomed to thinking of that hand as the *right* hand. Follow the same procedure but use green construction paper for the left hand.

When the children are wearing *both* red and green hands, teach them this little rhyme:

My right hand is red,
My left hand is green,
I'm the funniest boy (or girl)
You ever have seen!

18. Fun with Red Hands and Green Hands

Wear the red and green hands when doing this exercise, so children can do it correctly.

Swing arms, right then left,
Now touch your *right* shoe.
Swing arms right, then left,
Now touch your *left* knee.
Swing arms right, then left,
Now whirl around.
Swing arms right, then left,
And touch the ground.

Swing arms left, then right,
Now lift them high.
Swing arms left, then right,
Now bend the *left* knee.
Hold both hands out
In front of you.
Lift your *right* foot
And touch your *left* hand.
Lift your *left* foot
Touch your *right* hand.
Lift the right leg, then the left leg.
On the *right* leg stand.
Lift the left leg, then the right leg.
On the *left* leg stand.

19. Clapping Exercise

Stand with feet apart.
Jump in, jump out.
Jump in, jump out.
Now clap your hands.

Hands on hips.
Bend right, bend left.
Bend right, bend left.
Bend right, bend left.
Now clap your hands.

Arms above heads.
Squat down, stretch tall.
Squat down, stretch tall.
Squat down, stretch tall.
Now clap your hands.

20. Windmill

Position: On knees, body upright, arms outstretched.
Repeat the instructions as the children do this exercise five times.

Bend to the right
And touch the floor.
Bend to the left
And touch the floor.

21. This exercise is to be done to the tune of "Swing Low, Sweet Chariot."

Swing right, both boys and girls,
Swing right and stand up tall.
Swing right, both girls and boys,
Swing right and stand up tall.

Repeat, only start "Swing left---"
Jump left, both girls and boys,
Jump left and touch your toes.
Jump left, both girls and boys,
Jump left and touch your toes.

Repeat, only start "Jump right---"
Touch right foot, both girls and boys,
Touch right and bend your knee.
Touch right foot, both girls and boys,
Touch and bend your knee.

Repeat, only start "Touch left--"
Bend to left and swing to right,
Bend to left and swing to right.
Hands up high, bend down to left toe,
Hands up high, bend down to right toe.

Repeat, only start "Bend to right---"

Relaxing Exercises

22. Bouncing Balls

Position: Children sit in a double circle with plenty of room between each child.

Spread the legs along the floor, as far as they will go. Stretch the arms out in front.

Touch the *left* toe with both hands. *Bounce* the hands and torso, one, two, three, four.

Bend forward, and touch the spot directly in front with outstretched hands. *Bounce,* one, two, three, four.

Touch the right toe with both hands. *Bounce,* one, two, three, four.

23. Lefts and Rights

To play this game let each child put a dab of red poster paint on his right thumb and a dab of green paint on his left thumb.

Each child must listen carefully and follow *all* directions.

Arrange children in a line, one behind the other. Appoint three children to act as "watchers." Any child who fails to follow directions must sit on the floor to one side for the rest of the game.

Remind children that their right foot is on the same side as their right hand.

Give these directions slowly:

> Bend *right,* swing both arms to the *left.*
> Hop forward two hops on the *right* leg.
> Wave the *left* arm.
> Lift the *left* leg, and so on.

Let children sit in a circle and play a similar game with their painted thumbs, a "Simon Says" game. This time the children who don't follow directions must stand up.

Vary the directions. Begin:

> Simon says, "Thumbs up!"
> Simon says, "Thumbs down!"
> Thumbs down!

Simon says, "Right thumb up!"
Simon says, "Right thumb up!"
Left thumb down!

Simon says, "Left thumb hides."
    (cover it with the fingers)
Simon says, "Left thumb up!"
Right thumb hides!

Continue *Simon Says* by letting children think of ways to trick the players.

Kindergartners adore this relaxing, left-right game.

24. Bending Exercise

Turn around, touch the floor.
Stand up tall, touch once more.
Touch your toes, first left, then right.
Touch them again, with all your might.
Stretch your arms above your head.
Don't put them down, twirl around instead.
With hands on hips, jump out, then in.
Stand up tall and do a spin.
Touch the floor, *don't bend* your knees!
Walk your fingers, one, two, three.
Walk them back, one, two, three.
Stand up and stretch if you please!

25. Bunny Hop

Hop forward, one, two, three,
Hop backward, one, two, three.
Hop on the left foot, one, two, three,
Hop on the right foot, one, two, three.
Make one big jump with both your feet.
Now! All the bunnies run and hide!
    (Children return to tables.)

chapter ten

16 Delightful Activities That Help Children Express Creative Ideas

1. A "Creations" Box

Keep a cardboard box with smaller boxes fitted into it on a table where children can reach it. In the boxes keep old buttons, pieces of ribbon and braid, bits of yarn and small pieces of bright cloth; keep some pumpkin seeds and corn kernels; small pebbles and small sea shells; small pine cones and interesting seed pods from plants; tiny artificial flowers; felt, feathers, scraps of leather or bright plastic-coated cloth; scraps of fur or fur cloth and bits of fringe. Include in this box shiny paper from old Christmas cards; small paper or plastic doilies; bits of colored glass; ribbon and thread spools; crepe paper and tinfoil pans. Parents can help their kindergartners to keep this "creations" box filled with interesting materials.

Beside this box keep a stack of construction paper in many colors; a jar of paste and a tube of white glue.

The teacher will need to explain the uses of some of these materials. She should remind the children that they are there in the box for the use of *every* child in the room, regardless of who brought the materials to school. They will have to be reminded that the materials must be shared and that each child uses only those things that he *needs* to make a pretty picture.

Ask a few children to work together to make the first "creation" from materials in the box. Explain that all *creations* made by the children will be kept for several days. At a specified time each week the class can choose the "Creation of the Week." It will be displayed in a special place and the others can be displayed around it. Kindergartners will want to take these works of art home.

A "creations" box is a valuable asset in a kindergarten room when the teacher encourages children to use it freely to express their creative ideas. Underprivileged children find delight in the colors and textures of unfamiliar materials. Slow learners often find great pleasure in creating pictures and objects with these materials. Praise from their classmates helps to build up their self-esteem.

2. Block Creatures (See Figure 10-1)

Wooden building blocks, which are usually part of a kindergarten classroom's equipment, can be used for this activity. If there are no building blocks, the teacher will have to have wooden blocks cut, or use any scraps of lumber that are at least two inches thick and will stand on end.

If blocks are cut, a "two by four" from a lumberyard should be sawed into 3½", 4", 5", and 6" pieces. The ends of these blocks will be rough, but kindergartners will enjoy sanding them with course sandpaper to smooth them.

Making "creatures" out of the blocks can be a class activity or an individual activity. If kindergartners work together they should decide what storybook characters they would like to make. In the story that kindergartners love, "The Country Bunny and The Little Gold Shoes," by Dubose Heyward, the little brown country mother rabbit and her twenty-one children could all be made with blocks, as well as the Grandfather Bunny, the Jackrabbits and other characters.

Divide the class into groups and ask each group to make story characters from a story of its own choice. Provide children with construction paper and materials from the "creations" box of odds and ends, which should be a part of every kindergarten classroom.

Children can make features, arms, feet, paws, clothes and hats. Bunny ears can stick up through the hats. Suggest to them that feet or paws should be made long enough to protrude from beneath the block character.

Rabbit

Pig

Duck

Lady Rabbit

FIGURE 10-1 BLOCK CREATURES

Kindergartners will enjoy making and playing with these characters. When they tire of them, they can once more become ordinary blocks by stripping off the paper clothes and features.

3. Use Broken Crayons for Creative Designs and Pictures

Materials needed for this activity:

Broken pieces of crayon with paper coverings removed.
Small aluminum tins, empty tuna or other tin cans as receptacles in which to melt crayons.
Popsicle sticks or tongue depressors.

Paste brushes or large poster-paint brushes.

9" x 12" rectangles of corrugated paper, cut on a paper cutter.

An electric hot plate for melting crayons.

A table, covered with heavy plastic cloth, oilcloth, or newspapers.

How to make the pictures: Give children construction paper and ask them to draw simple pictures or designs. These should be colored *very* lightly with not more than three colors. Paste each of these pictures to a corrugated piece of cardboard.

The teacher will have ready the melted crayons in red, blue, brown, black, green, orange, yellow and purple. She should show the children how to apply the melted crayon. The paste or paintbrush is dipped into the melted crayon and is used to carefully paint *inside* the lines of the picture or design. As the melted crayon cools, show the kindergartners how to use the Popsicle sticks or tongue depressors to "build up" the colors on their pictures. This is done by gently pushing the cooling crayon wax toward the center of the picture and roughing it with the wooden stick. Apply melted crayon several times to the same area for the proper buildup of the wax.

Children should work in groups using the melted wax as it is ready. After all the needed colors have been applied let the picture "harden" as the wax cools.

The next day the children can outline their pictures or designs with black crayon. This technique is enjoyed by kindergartners. It makes unusual pictures to display and to take home.

4. Crayon-painted Butterflies

Teacher's preparation: Use a razor blade, knife or vegetable grater to make shavings of broken crayons.

Provide pieces of waxed paper.

Provide an iron.

Cover a flat surface with newspapers, or brown paper.

Child's preparation: The teacher should show children how to fold paper, then cut butterfly shapes on the folded edge. Lay these butterflies aside for later use.

Give each child two pieces of waxed paper. One at a time the children come to the table and sprinkle shavings of several colors on one of their waxed paper sheets. The area should be completely covered to within an inch or more of the edges, but the shavings should not be piled up in any area. Cover the crayon with the other sheet of waxed paper. The teacher presses the two sheets together with a warm iron, until all the shavings between them have melted. Set them aside to cool.

When all the children have finished with their papers, tell them to gently fold the "painted" sheet in half; then the folded butterfly pattern is placed along the fold of waxed paper. They should trace around these patterns, then cut out the butterflies.

A slim black body can be colored on both sides of the waxed paper if the butterfly is to hang in a window or as part of a mobile. Antennae can be pasted on, if the child desires.

The beautifully colored, transparent butterflies are now ready to be put on display in the room. They can be mounted on colored construction paper, to be displayed in the room or in a hall; they can be used for mobiles; they can be hung in windows as bright and beautiful decorations; and they can be used on a bulletin board. Some children may prefer to wear them as lapel pins.

Note: Fall leaves can be made in the same way as the butterflies were made. Use leaf shapes of many kinds and cut leaves out of the waxed paper that has been "painted" with melted crayons. Children can put in stems and veins of leaves with dark green or black crayons.

For Christmas trees, use green shavings, with touches of vivid colors here and there for "lights." Have children cut their own fir tree patterns on folded paper.

5. A Do-it-yourself Playhouse

This playhouse can be made from any number of *large* cardboard cartons. It can have rooms with four sides and doors between (which children can crawl through), or it can be open on one side, to accommodate housekeeping toys.

Where to find boxes: First check with kindergarten parents to see if a father, uncle or friend has large paper boxes on hand, or knows of a source where they could be obtained. The teacher can contact paint stores or lumberyards that stock unpainted furniture, which comes packed in large cartons. She can ask the stores to save the boxes for school use. When several boxes have been acquired, let kindergartners plan how the boxes must be fitted together to make the kind of a house they want. Use very long paper fasteners to hold the boxes together. Use wide masking tape or pasted newspaper strips to cover all joining seams.

Kindergartners should decide where doors and windows need to be located. The teacher should cut the openings. Use a razor blade or very sharp knife. Cut down through the center of a window opening, cut across the top and the bottom, then fold the cardboard back on each side for shutters. These can be closed.

Paint the playhouse. Trim the door and window openings. Add curtains made from cloth or paper.

Children can make paper flowers for window boxes. Use shoe boxes for these and fasten them on with paste. Reinforce them with paper fasteners.

6. Rhythm Instruments Children Can Make

The average kindergarten room is usually lacking in enough musical or rhythm instruments for each student to have one to use.

Children can make their own drums and rattles, as well as other rhythm instruments.

Materials that can be used:

Tin cans with lids. (Shortening or others)
Coffee cans, with plastic lids.
Small plastic containers.
Aluminum foil pie tins, of various sizes, including tart tins.
½" dowel sticks (from hardware stores), cut into 12" lengths for rhythm sticks.
Use 3/8" dowel sticks, with crutch tips (also from hardware stores) for drum beaters.

How to make the instruments. Decorate the sides of tin cans with paper, paint, tape, fringe and so on. These, with their *tin* lids, make drums with a particular sound. This sound can be varied by using several kinds of "beaters." A hairbrush, wooden stick or a dowel stick with a crutch tip on one end all make good drum beaters when applied to tin drums, but the sounds are not alike.

Use paint, paper, or Contac paper to decorate tin coffee cans. Open *both* ends and cover them with plastic lids. Attach these lids with glue so they cannot be removed. These cans make good bongo drums and are beaten with the hands.

Fill small plastic containers with beans, corn or small stones to use as rattles. Fasten the lids on with tape. Decorate them with items from the "creations" box.

Before the lids are fastened on the rattles, let children experiment with the sounds made by a *few* objects inside the container, as compared to the sounds made by *many* objects. Let them decide how full of stones, beans or corn the containers should be.

Aluminum foil tins can be fastened together around the edges with a stapler, *after* the corn kernels or beans have been put inside. Decorate the edges.

Large pie tins (with nothing inside) can be fastened together and used like a tambourine. Sounds are made on the tins' surfaces by striking them with the hands.

Buy enough ½" dowel sticks so several children can each have two rhythm sticks. They should be at least 10" in length. They can be stained, varnished, lacquered or painted.

Blocks of scrap wood, clapped together, can also be used as rhythm instruments.

Buy dowel sticks and enough crutch tips to fit one end of each "beater" needed. Use these for drums with tin or plastic ends.

7. Gifts for Mothers

A few weeks before this activity begins, send notes home with kindergartners, asking their mothers to save spray can tops from furniture wax, polish, paint, hair spray and so on. Small cans such as pimento, Vienna sausage, tuna and so on, are also acceptable for this activity.

Provide children with white glue and let them decorate one

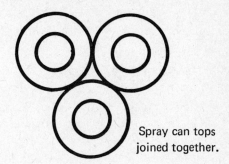

Spray can tops
joined together.

FIGURE 10-3
DECORATED CAN

FIGURE 10-2

or more cans in any way they like. They can use lace, braid, beads, or they can make their own decorations.

If the supply of plastic tops is ample, show the children how to glue two or three can lids together. (See Figure 10-2) In a set of three a small figure made of paper, plastic or china, can be put on top at the point where the cans meet.

Can tops with small circles inside them make nice, low candleholders. Can lids without the circle can be used to display a single flower, to hold pins, buttons, paper clips and other small items.

These decorated, colorful plastic can tops make nice Mother's Day gifts. (See Figure 10-3)

8. Three Recipes for Clay Kindergartners Can Make

Recipe 1

1 part salt
4 parts flour
Enough water to moisten

Knead the mixture on a board that has been covered with waxed paper. Roll with a wooden rolling pin into a flat surface using a little more flour if necessary. This dough, or clay can be molded with the fingers into shapes.

Recipe 2

1 cup water
1 cup flour

1 cup salt

1 tablespoon powdered alum

Mix the ingredients together. Knead on waxed paper using more flour if necessary. Roll out or shape, as in Recipe 1.

Recipe 3: Basic recipe

3 slices *white* bread. Cut off crusts and break bread into small pieces.

3 teaspoons, or more, of Elmer's Glue-All.

1 teaspoon glycerine.

3 drops lemon juice (optional).

Mix these ingredients together into a smooth dough.

Roll dough between two waxed papers, or shape with hands.

Allow objects made to dry twenty-four hours before spraying them with clear lacquer.

If the clay in these three recipes needs to be tinted, use cake coloring, adding it to the mixture before it is rolled out or shaped. Use cookie cutters of various shapes to cut the rolled-out clay. Smooth the edges with water-moistened fingers. Allow the shapes to dry before painting.

When small animals are made from this clay, short pipe cleaners can be rolled inside the body and head parts and into the legs. This will make the body easier to shape and the legs more substantial.

Kindergartners can punch holes in these clay objects and use them for Christmas tree decorations. They can suspend them from bent coat hangers or bamboo rods and use them as mobiles. They can also make large, flat figures of owls, faces and so on, hang them close together from a bamboo rod and use them for "clackers" in the schoolroom or at home.

Storybook characters can be made from these clays. A group of flat shapes, representing *all* the characters in one story, would make a good group activity. Painted and lacquered, they could be used on a bulletin board, then become part of the kindergarten room equipment.

These clays are excellent to use for making artificial fruit sections for math games. They can be used for geometric shapes, for small bowls and trays.

9. Designs with Geometric Shapes

This creative activity can accompany math experiences or can be used as an art project.

Provide children with colored paper, squares, triangles of all sizes and rectangles, all of which can be cut on a paper cutter. They should be cut from oaktag or cardboard. They are used as patterns. Cut cardboard circles, also to be used as patterns. Children should trace around the patterns, then cut their own geometric figures from their favorite colored paper.

When all this material is ready, let each child choose the color for the picture background and arrange the geometric figures in his own design. Children make very attractive engines, cars, flower arrangements, candleholders with candles, houses and abstract designs with colored geometric shapes.

Dramatizations and Role-playing

10. Can You Guess Who I Am?

Note: This dramatic-play game should not be introduced until kindergartners are quite familiar with many stories and their characters.

The Game: Briefly discuss with the class the following stories, from which children may want to choose characters for dramatization: "Peter Rabbit," "Peter Pan," "Jack and Jill," "Little Bo-Peep," "Rumpelstiltskin," "The Owl and The Pussycat," "Three Billy Goats Gruff," "Little Red Riding Hood," "Jack and the Beanstalk," "Goldilocks and the Three Bears," "Snow White," "Cinderella," "Pinocchio," and "The Three Little Pigs" are some stories that become familiar to kindergartners and are easy to play.

Explain that each child is to think of a character in one of these stories and *act out* the part of the character. He will then ask, "Can you guess who I am?" If nobody guesses, the child may give three clues, one at a time, giving his classmates time to "guess who" after each clue. The child who guesses correctly may present his own characterization next.

The hints, or clues, should not mention *names,* but can be as explicit as "I smell the blood of an Englishman." Peter Rabbit could ask for camomile tea and so on.

Allow each child in the room to take part in these dramatizations. After each has played a character alone, several children may want to work as a group and dramatize an entire story. If so, plan the event for another day. Encourage the group to use props and to make simple costumes, if possible.

11. Three-Sided Cardboard Costumes That Can Be Folded and Stored

Use sides of corrugated paper boxes or pieces of oaktag. Cut one piece long enough to cover the average kindergartner from neck to knees. Cut two more pieces the same length as the first, but wide enough to meet in the back when joined on each side to the first piece. The three pieces of cardboard will form a triangle when worn by a child. (See Figure 10-4)

The cardboard pieces can be fastened together in two ways: (a) Punch two or three holes in each of the cardboards, along the edges. Used gummed reinforcements on both sides so the holes will not tear out. Use string to tie the cardboard pieces together. (b) The cardboards can be fastened by using 2½" masking tape. Hold the edges so they do not *quite* touch. Cover with tape on *both* sides of the cardboards. The pieces will bend freely at the taped edges but will not tear.

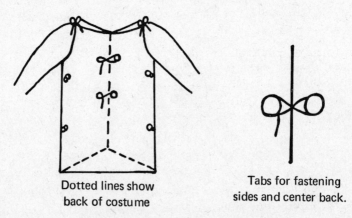

Dotted lines show
back of costume

Tabs for fastening
sides and center back.

FIGURE 10-4 CARDBOARD COSTUME

Adjust the cardboard costume to the child by letting him try it on. Mark the places where holes must be cut for the child's arms. Tape around these holes to keep the paper from tearing. Make the two back parts narrower, if necessary, so they will *just* meet. The edges can be tied, as suggested for the sides. An easier way for children to fasten them is to use the tab and string method. (Figure 10-4)

Children can paint the costumes. They can then be stored in a neat stack and will take up little space.

Masks or head coverings can be made of paper bags. (See Figure 10-5)

Allow children to use these costumes for dramatizations during free-play time.

12. Story-character Costumes Kindergartners Can Make

Ask children to bring in boxes of all sizes. Use them to make heads and bodies for storybook-character costumes.

The head-boxes should be opened at one end. Cut eye

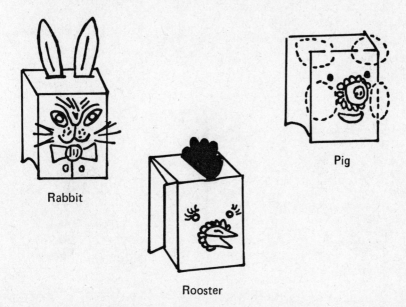

Rabbit

Pig

Rooster

FIGURE 10-5 MASKS MADE FROM BAGS

holes and a hole for a mouth. Animal heads can have whiskers of broom straws or pipe cleaners. Ears can be made out of paper and attached with glue. Imitation leather or flexible plastic make good ears. Hair or manes can be made from straw, yarn or raveled-out rope. A snout for a pig can be a tin can attached to the box with masking tape.

Open the body-box to enclose the child's body. Cut holes on the sides for arms. Children can paint the costumes. Put fasteners on the back like those in Figure 10-5 so children can fasten them for each other.

Papier-mâché Projects

13. Easter Eggs

This project should be started at least a month before Easter. It will take some time to complete. While it is essentially an activity to encourage creative expression in each child, it is also a group activity that is valuable in *many* areas of learning.

Kindergartners learn new manipulative skills. They must listen for directions and carefully follow them when making the eggs. They must use patience with a project that will take more than a day or two to complete. They must learn to share materials and to show consideration for the rights and needs of their classmates.

Bandaged egg-shape

Cut through
the center
of the egg

Scene inside egg

FIGURE 10-6

Materials needed:

Egg-shaped hosiery packages or very *large* lemons
Soft paper towels, torn into bits; or newspaper torn into bits
Strips of newspaper or from *firm* paper towels
A bag of wallpaper paste
Poster paints

Send notes home with kindergartners some time before the project starts asking mothers (and friends) to save the hosiery packages for this egg-making project.

How to make the eggs (See Figure 10-6)

Explain to the children that the eggs are to be made with *papier-mâché.* This is pronounced "pa pyā´ ma shā´" and comes from two French words meaning *paper* and *masticate.* When food is masticated it is chewed, so papier-mâché means *chewed* paper! (Kindergartners enjoy interesting information about things they do and they will like knowing the meaning of this new word.)

Of course the kindergartners will not actually chew the paper towels or newpapers they use, but they will tear them into tiny pieces. These pieces should be covered with water and soaked for several days, until the paper softens. For a large class there should be at least a half-gallon of prepared papier-mâché pulp.

Squeeze the water out of the wet paper. Add dry paper paste to the paper until it feels doughy. Add a littly water if it becomes too stiff. The "dough" should be moist and pliable. The pulp can be mixed with the paste in small quantities, so kindergartners can do the mixing.

Tightly cover the papier-mâché or wrap in waxed paper, put it in a cool place, and allow it set for a few days before using it.

Plastic egg-shaped hosiery packages or large lemons will serve as molds for the papier-mâché eggs. Cover the molds with "Vaseline" Petroleum Jelly or another good lubricant. Later, when the outer covering is dry, it is cut in half so the center shape or mold can be removed and used over and over again. The lubricant makes it possible to easily remove the paper covering.

After the lubricant is applied to the mold, it must be "bandaged" all over with several thicknesses of towel or newspaper strips dipped in wallpaper paste. This paste is made by mixing the dry powder with water to the consistency of white sauce or very thick cream.

Important: Since the halves of one whole egg are to be shared by two children, kindergartners should work in pairs for the next egg-making tasks.

Dip the towel or newspaper strips in the paste, slide the excess paste off with the fingers, then apply the strips first vertically, then crisscross them with horizontal strips so that there are at least three thicknesses of "bandage."

Set the eggs aside to dry for several days. When thoroughly dry, the teacher uses a razor blade or sharp knife to cut the egg shapes in half. A half shape is given to each child in the room. If enough molds are not available to make the required amount of eggs at one time, let new groups start work on another supply of papier-mâché eggs. Wait until all have been dried and divided before starting the class on decorating them.

Show the children how to *lightly* cover their half-eggs with the paper pulp, inside and out. The papier-mâché is applied with the hands, in a thin coat, using only a small amount at a time. Remind the children to handle the half-eggs carefully, as they may bend out of shape with the weight of the wet paper pulp. Hold the egg in one hand, dip the fingers of the other hand in water, then gently smooth the surface until there are no rough spots.

Smooth a place at the bottom of each half-egg. Set each upright to dry. Egg cartons or muffin tins make good containers to set them in. Let the eggs dry for several days. When dry, glue the base of the egg to the top of a can lid, to a large button, or to several cardboard disks that have been pasted together. Let dry.

Paint the inside and outside of the egg with poster paint. If a child wants pastel colors, show him how to get the desired tints. Paint the bases of the eggs.

Perhaps the teacher will want to suggest ways in which the child can make his egg interesting and beautiful, both inside and out. The inside can be an Easter scene, with the picture of a yellow baby chick, a white or brown rabbit, or a basket of eggs and flowers. A child may have some small plastic figure he would like to put into his egg. He can use small artificial flowers or make flowers himself.

Always let the child choose his decorations and put them on himself.

Use white glue on objects that are to go inside the egg. Buttons, beads, and plastic objects may need to be put on with plastic glue. Paste can be used to attach braids, lace, paper flowers, or other decorations.

When the half-eggs are finished they are truly beautiful and should be displayed in the school, if possible, so other children can enjoy them. They can be taken home. They can be suspended from a piece of bamboo and displayed in the room as a mobile. They can be used on an Easter egg tree.

14. Large Papier-mâché Eggs with Peepholes, and Scenes Inside

This is a class project.

Very large Easter eggs can be made in the same way as the half eggs were made. The "mold," over which the egg is made, is a large oval balloon.

Follow the same steps in preparing the materials for the large eggs as were followed for the half-eggs. Bandage the balloon surface first, however, since the balloon will be collapsed in this project and will come out easily.

Let the class decide what the scene inside the egg will be. Should the egg be made so it will stand on end, or lie on its side? The position of the egg will determine where the peephole is to be cut in the egg shape.

Make the cutting off-center, all around the egg. The peephole will be cut later. Paint the larger part of the egg and arrange the scene in it. Cut the peephole in the smaller part. Paint it inside.

Fasten the two egg pieces together by "bandaging" over the cut edges with strips of paper towel or newspaper. Allow this to dry thoroughly.

Decorate the opening of the egg with lace, braid, or fringe. Decorate the outside. Fasten the large egg to a base (a box, bowl, or several layers of corrugated paper pasted together will do), and set it on a table, or suspend it at a child's eye level.

Kindergartners help make these large eggs, but they never seem to tire of "taking a peek" to see what is inside!

15. Paper Animals

These animals will be sturdy enough to play with at school and to take home. Some kindergartners do not have the skills or the patience to make animals that cannot be completed in one or two activity periods. Those children can make alligators, or other simple creatures. Most children accept the challenge of making four-legged animals and will even use wire, with the teacher's assistance, to make the bodies and legs firm.

Materials needed:

Newspapers
Paper bags of all sizes
Cord
Masking tape
Dry wallpaper paste
Long pipe cleaners and flower-stem wire. (Can be purchased at a
    hobby or notions store)
Wire hangers
Pliers

How to make simple animals. Roll newspapers the long way into rolls and tie in several places with cord. Masking tape can be used instead of cord. Wire twists that come in boxes of plastic bags are also useful for these paper rolls. Little fingers can manage them better than cord.

An alligator. If children want to make alligators, they start with a long roll of newspaper, stuff a small paper bag with bits of paper, tie the end, then tie the bag around the middle of the first paper roll. Bandage with paste-covered newspaper strips all over the alligator shape. Cut two pieces of cardboard into triangular nose shapes and fasten to the head end for a snout. Glue on two small Styrofoam balls or round buttons for eyes. Cut four paper legs and paste them to the alligator body. Paint the body with poster paint. (See Figure 10-7)

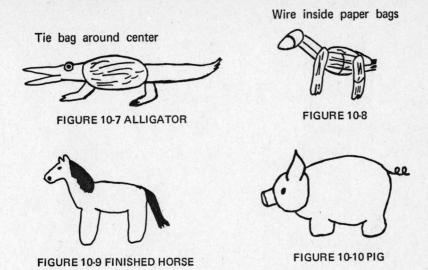

Tie bag around center

FIGURE 10-7 ALLIGATOR

Wire inside paper bags

FIGURE 10-8

FIGURE 10-9 FINISHED HORSE

FIGURE 10-10 PIG

Four-legged animals. Put a piece of wire, cut from a wire hanger or a piece of flower-stem wire, inside a long roll of newspaper and fasten the roll in several places. Paste paper across the ends to keep the wire from sliding out. Bend for a body and head. (See Figure 10-8)

Make two more rolls of paper, with wire inside, to use for legs. Tape to the body. Tie a very small paper-stuffed sack to the head end. A ball of crushed paper can also be attached to the end with pasted strips to serve as a head.

Bandage the entire body. Attach ears and tail before painting. Paint the eyes and mouth. If the animal is a horse, add a mane made from yarn or frayed rope. (Figure 10-9)

When making a pig, attach crushed balls of paper towel to each side of the head before bandaging for jaws. Tie a crushed paper-filled sack around the middle of the animal. Tape a round tin can to the head for a nose. After the pig's body is bandaged, paste on ears that come to a point but tip over, and attach curled pipe cleaner for a tail. (Figure 10-10)

Important. If individual animal-making is too complicated for a particular group of kindergartners, make the project a group activity in which all can share. A zoo can be built for the room with open enclosures for some animals and paper cages for others. Animals for a pet shop can also be made.

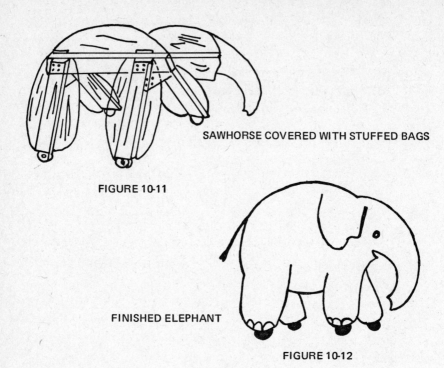

SAWHORSE COVERED WITH STUFFED BAGS

FIGURE 10-11

FINISHED ELEPHANT

FIGURE 10-12

16. An Elephant to Ride.

Animals large enough to ride can be made as a group activity. This elephant is sturdy enough to become part of the room equipment for a time.

A sawhorse must be used as a base for the elephant. This can probably be borrowed, for a time, from some child's father. When the animal is dismantled the sawhorse can be returned to its owner. Have ball-bearing rollers put on the sawhorse so it can be wheeled around the room. A piece of wood should be nailed to the front of the sawhorse, to serve as a base for the elephant's head.

How to make the elephant's body. Fill *large* paper sacks *solidly* with newspapers and tape the ends securely. Tie as many bags as needed around the middle of the sawhorse for the elephant's body. Tie smaller stuffed sacks around the head piece and around the four legs of the sawhorse. (See Figure 10-11)

Cover a long piece of wire with rolled newspapers for a trunk. Make it thicker at one end than the other. Cover the ends well. Attach the trunk to the elephant head with tape or paste-covered strips of newspaper. Bandage the elephant's entire body with *many* layers of pasted newspaper strips. Do this over a period of several days, letting a few layers dry, then adding a few more. The last layers should be smoothed down with water-moistened fingers, or the palms of hands. This animal will not have a coating of paper pulp.

Attach floppy ears and a rope tail. Paint the elephant. Poster paint will do, but enamel is better for an animal that children will ride. Last of all add eyes and toes. (See Figure 10-12)

If ridden with care this elephant will last a long time. It will furnish the children with many hours of pleasure.

Conclusion

This *Kindergarten Teacher's Activities Desk Book* has offered a collection of easily usable materials that cover a wide range of kindergartners' interests.

These activities, projects, and games-that-teach were selected to help all young children develop their maximum learning potentials and to find satisfaction in acquiring skills commensurate with their individual abilities.

The author sincerely hopes that these ideas and methods will help kindergartners to achieve new levels of learning. The very wide range of subject material should help them to enjoy their world and to become more aware of the contribution they can make as young, well-informed, and interested citizens.

Index